Home Built Discipline

Raymond & Dorothy Moore

with

Dennis Moore & Kathleen Kordenbrock

THOMAS NELSON PUBLISHERS

Nashville • Camden • Kansas City

ADULT BOOKS BY THE AUTHORS:

Home Grown Kids
Home Spun Schools
Home Style Teaching
Home Made Health
Better Late than Early
School Can Wait

CHILDREN'S BOOKS BY THE AUTHORS:

Guess Who Took the Battered-up Bike
Quit? Not Me!
Oh, No! Miss Dent Is Coming to Dinner

Published in Nashville, Tennessee, by Thomas Nelson, Inc., and distributed in Canada by Lawson Falle, Ltd., Cambridge, Ontario.

Printed in the United States of America.

Library of Congress Cataloging-in-publication Data

Moore, Raymond S.
  Homebuilt discipline.

  1. Discipline of children.   2. Parenting.
I. Moore, Dorothy N.   II. Title.
ISBN 0-8407-3159-0

1 2 3 4 5 — 94 93 92 91 90

This book is dedicated to O. D. and Ruth McKee, who did a much better than average job in disciplining their kids and who have led in the development of the Hewitt Research Foundation and the Hewitt-Moore Child Development Center, with Mr. McKee as charter member of the Hewitt Board and chairman for six years. And to present and past members of that board who made strong positive contributions to Hewitt.

◣◣◣◣◣◣◣◣◣◣◣◣◣ Contents ◢◢◢◢◢◢◢◢◢◢◢◢◢

Enjoy Those Wet Oatmeal Kisses
While You Can

The baby is teething. The children are fighting. Your husband just called and said, "Eat dinner without me."

One of these days you'll explode and shout to the kids, "Why don't you grow up and act your age?" And they will.

Or: "You guys get outside and find yourselves something to do. And don't slam the door!" And they don't.

You'll straighten their bedrooms all neat and tidy, toys displayed on the shelf, hangers in the closet, animals caged. You'll yell, "Now I want it to stay this way!" And it will.

You will prepare a perfect dinner with a salad that hasn't had all the olives picked out and a cake with no finger traces in the icing, and you'll say: "Now THIS is a meal for company." And you will eat it alone.

You'll yell, "I want complete privacy on the phone. No screaming. Do you hear me?" And no one will answer.

No more plastic tablecloths stained with spaghetti. No more dandelion bouquets. No more iron-on patches. No more wet, knotted shoelaces, muddy boots, or rubber bands for ponytails.

Imagine. A lipstick with a point. No baby sitter for New Year's Eve, washing clothes only once a week, no PTA meetings or silly school plays where your child is a tree. No carpools, blaring stereos, forgotten lunch money.

No more Christmas presents made of library paste and tooth-picks. No wet oatmeal kisses. No more tooth fairy. No more giggles in the dark, scraped knees to kiss, or sticky fingers to clean. Only a voice asking: "Why don't you grow up?"

And the silence echoes: "I DID."

—Author Unknown

This book is written by two professionals with a combined experience of more than 140 years of discipline and being disciplined. As might be expected, the male is far more experienced in both giving and getting discipline. If you want a bit of verification, you might read the last chapter first. At that time I thought that all discipline was punishment. Now I know better.

Discipline should be an exciting, creative experience rather than punishment. In fact, discipline is training of the most fundamental kind. Wise, happy parents are sculptors who shape young lives, molding them into beautiful vessels. The goal is to form exciting, altruistic, constructive family members into self-worthy, self-directed neighbors who love others as much as themselves.

Both of us have been specialists in discipline as heads of families, home schools, preschools, classrooms, school systems (public and parochial), colleges or both. We have received enough letters from people like you to sense that the time is ripe for a *commonsense* book that can help both parents and teachers keep an even keel in home and classroom, especially if it helps them understand how children develop and learn. You will find some uncommon ideas, but they will prove themselves in practice if you have the love, courage, and consistency to go all the way.

This book will help you develop behavior patterns in you and your children. It will help you avoid pitfalls by showing you in advance where these stumbling places are.

Two of our children, Dennis and Kathleen, both of them

teachers and developmental psychologists who have a special way with children, went through our manuscript and added some of the more sparkling ideas. We are honored to add our children as collaborators.

PART ONE

DISCIPLINE AS DISCIPLESHIP

A Commonsense Guide to Discipline

Recently our guests were a young professional couple with two boys, James and John, ages five and three. Their names may seem common enough, but the little boys were anything but ordinary. James was highly organized, whether he was playing with LEGO Bricks or filling the dishwasher or helping his parents pack their car.

John was one of the most cognitively mature three-year-olds we have met; his reasoning was well advanced for his age. He did not yet have much interest in organization, but he was always evaluating situations or people or things. He was a real charmer. Often he came around to tell us how much he enjoyed being with us. He would say, "I love you, but I like you, too." And he would compliment a shirt or blouse, anything which pleased his genuine sensitivity and creativity. Both boys were very bright and better behaved than most youngsters their ages.

Yet it became apparent early in their visit that both of them had a problem that made their father unhappy and was wearing their mother out. When their parents asked them to run an errand or get dressed or wash or eat with good manners, they often stalled. Sometimes they were downright obstinate or discourteous. When their mother offered them a fresh tomato and lettuce salad with carrot and celery sticks on the side, James protested. And John echoed, "I don't like carrots either!" At that point their mother, both palms up in a silent appeal for help, turned to my wife.

The boys, apparently victorious, saw her.

Dorothy leaned both of her elbows on the high kitchen counter and held her face on her hands, looking directly at the boys who sat on tall chairs on the other side.

"Would you like me to tell you a story?" she smiled, arching eyebrows already arched high by nature.

"Yes!" responded James, and John quickly echoed, "Yeah, I'd like it."

"Well," she began, "when my children were little, they tried to tell me what they would eat and wouldn't eat and what they would do and wouldn't do. So I had a plan. Would you like to know what it was?"

"Yeah," John enthused, always curious. James was not so sure, but both listened attentively.

"If my children said they didn't want any carrots, I never argued with them." The boys smiled knowingly at their mother who stood near my wife. "I told them they didn't have to eat the carrots now."

The boys' grins widened.

Then my wife added, "I told them they could get down from the table."

James frowned. "Then when did they eat?"

"At the next meal."

"No more food?"

"No more food until the next meal, not even a snack."

"Not even a snack . . ." came the echo from the three-year-old, who looked first at Dorothy, then at his big brother.

"Mama," said John, lifting a carrot stick, "I like carrots."

James quickly joined him. "I like everything you fix."

That brief exchange set off one of the smoothest weekends we have ever had with a family of children. My wife had an advantage, of course, since she was not with the boys every day (there is nothing wrong with parents using other adults discreetly). But the boys were obviously impressed by Dorothy's decisiveness and the certainty and security that comes from such authority.

Prevention Rather Than Remedy

The best way to establish discipline in any situation—at home, in the classroom, on the playground, in the office, or elsewhere—is to get there before trouble starts, or at least before your tolerance turns to frustration. Select the simplest possible solution that is right and true and carry it out with consistency. This solution may not be perfect, but it is the best within your framework of experience. And you will learn more by experience, much more.

You will do your children no favor to allow them to grow up undisciplined. Those who are allowed to have their own way are restless, discontent, and insecure—like a ship without a rudder, tossed by the wind and waves of expediency. Lack of discipline is the most common complaint of teachers who indicate its serious interference with their goals in the classroom. Parents, too, find ways to get obnoxious children out of their way as much as possible, hoping the problem will go away so they will not have to bother. Because undisciplined children are not likely to receive as much positive feedback and attention from adults as well-disciplined children, they are often hampered in mental development.

Both prevention and remedy of misbehavior generally follow identical principles. Prevention is a matter of utilizing these methods to plan ahead—before misbehavior. Remedy is using them after it starts.

Delinquency is often predicted by five social factors. The five factors are: (1) affection of father for the child, (2) discipline by the father, (3) affection of the mother for the child, (4) supervision and discipline by the mother, and (5) cohesiveness of the family.

More than any other influence, the education and circumstances of your children in their early, impressionable years determines the direction of their lives. If you fail to teach the basic lessons of respect, obedience and self-control, your home will crumble. A wise parent soon finds that prevention is a great insurance policy, available at a much lower price than remedy.

Plan ahead and work your plan. If more remedy is needed, it also pays to understand the principles . . . and your children! Among the best examples of such planning and follow-through we have ever seen were, of all things, two bald eagles.

Treetop Disciplinarians

Thirty miles or so up the Columbia River Gorge from our home, I watched the huge eagles as they laid plans for their young. I was staying alone for a few days at a dear friend's cabin to do some writing by a little mountain lake on the north side of the gorge. My host first pointed out the female, perched high on a cedar where the treetop had broken off or been mutilated years ago. She and later her mate were apparently freshening and strengthening an old nest, always cooperating and responding to each other, as they did later with their young.

Eventually the big birds found the nest secure enough to settle down and get ready to raise a family. They seemed as systematic as a skillfully programmed computer. They had done their work. Now they could rest and wait for the hatching, some weeks away.

Sure enough, a few weeks later, when some of us were again in the area, we watched through binoculars what appeared to be some scuffling in the nest. Shortly an eaglet was tipped out, and it fluttered toward the ground. The big eagle retrieved the birdling before it touched ground and took it higher into the sky where it again let it go, eventually bringing the little one back to the nest, encouraging him, then repeating the process with others of its young. After several days of this patient process, the exercise became more like play as the little birds were flying on their own. They had learned from the precise, consistent example and assistance of their parents.

Even then the parents remained on guard wherever the eaglets flew. The big birds had instinctive plans for every stage of their offspring's growth and were ready for every emergency, since they thoroughly understood the development of their young. The lives of those eaglets depended on the care and training given by their parents.

So with our children. Although parents have instincts, too, humans have an advantage: We are endowed with reason. Our responsibility for planning the deportment of our young is as much greater than the eagle's as reason is greater than instinct. Considering the length of human life, the time allowed for a child's training is brief at best. Hardly a week goes by that we don't hear parents or grandparents wish out loud that they had not let incidentals and minor preoccupations keep them from spending more time with their children.

The eagles were prepared at every turn. They instinctively thought ahead. For you and me age-old wisdom suggests that "a stitch in time saves nine" or "an ounce of prevention is worth a pound of cure." Although we are deeply concerned with remedy and will deal with it later in this book, wise parents plan ahead.

In general, mothers are the ones charged with the primary responsibilities of discipline because of their longer and closer association with their young children. Still, a father's support in helping a mother maintain a consistent, solid front is essential. Nothing is more confusing to a child or damaging to good discipline than parents who have conflicting disciplinary methods or points of view.

Building a Foundation

Read carefully the brief chapters in this book that cover your children's development. Make up your mind to proceed deliberately; buddy with your spouse, or with another single parent if you are now alone. Be optimistic, and watch the results!

Next, apply tested principles and methods on your children. It will take some character and determination to line them up in sound practices, which other families may ignore. For example, it will take courage to get your family to bed early when all the kids in the neighborhood are lounging around TV until all hours of the night. But your investment in determination now will pay off richly later. Commonsense scheduling may not always be easy, but it is tangible. You *can* do it, especially when you set the example.

Remember, also, that the basic framework for discipline is built in the first three years. Though all is not lost if your child is out of control, retrieval will be much more difficult, mostly because the errors of your techniques (or those of whoever is the responsible person) must be corrected. Usually problem children are created by problem adults, and only correction in the adult can change the child—with much more pain and frustration than would have been necessary earlier.

Controls That Bring Self-Discipline

So much for your own foundation. Now for building specific controls, which, whether for prevention or remedy, lead to sound discipline. There are at least ten building blocks that come nearer than others to making discipline pleasant and almost automatic. They are priceless, because love is priceless, and their price is an abundance of love. They are infinitely more effective than bribing or indulging your children. They will go a long way toward making deprivation and the switch unnecessary.

Part Three of this book will explore these building blocks fully. We lay them down here in the ten short chapters which follow. They are not necessarily arranged in order of importance, since all are crucial to a strong, pleasant program of discipline: (1) warm responsiveness and example; (2) routine, regularity, and order; (3) constructive work and play; (4) service to others; (5) camaraderie, courtesy, and communication; (6) consistency and unity; (7) learning how to think; (8) encouragement and appreciation, sometimes with rewards; (9) health, including diet, dress, sleep, and exercise; and (10) management of money.

Running down through all these short chapters is the strand of implicit authority. It will be weak or strong, depending on you, your understanding of your children and the way they develop, your consistency, your responsiveness, and your example. Children, like soldiers or office workers or students at school, should have only that freedom or authority for which they can handle equal or commensurate responsibility. You won't ask a two-year-old to start a fire in the stove or a ten-year-old to drive your car. You will be alert to their development and abilities, always monitoring to insure the authority-responsibility balance.

When remedy *is* necessary, deprivation of privileges and even a spanking will be better understood by children who know they are appreciated, for they trust you. The fact that you care enough to deal with them forthrightly and consistently impresses them clearly that you love them. Child license—freedom without responsibility—is no freedom at all. Children do not feel safe with you or that you care when you let them do whatever they want to do. In summary, the best of all roads to obedience and control is the one paved by parents who show love to one another—the father who offers kindly attention to the mother and the mother who shows loving respect to the father. We do not speak of sentimentality but of selfless affection based on mutual regard. This always builds self-respect and self-control in all members of the family. Children should learn such respect for parents and others from their earliest years, helping in every way they can to make life happier and more secure for others.

The lessons and example of the eagle are safe guides in

principle for you and your children. Their cooperation and responsiveness to each other, their instinctive order and routine, their constructive mixture of work and play, the consistency of their example, and their obvious encouragement of their young are worth our reflection and that of our children. Here we have the foundation for great discipline.

◼◼◼◼◼◼◼◼◼◼◼◼◼ 2 ◼◼◼◼◼◼◼◼◼◼◼◼◼
Discipleship

I remember as a youngster the "rambling four" formed by John and Billy Wells and my brother Charles and me. At one point Charles was about thirteen, John twelve, and Billy and I, eleven. Although John and Billy lived a good half mile away in the little California town of Montrose, we were together almost as much as if we lived next door. Charles was the moderate example, and Billy and I were the mischievous ones, particularly teasing girls and testing the teacher's patience in the little one-room school. John stood by Charles in making sure that things didn't go too far. Thus certain preadolescent ethics were assured: honesty and reasonable cleanliness of body and tongue, without any rigid demands that might grate on young nerves.

Billy and I often tested Charles and John without realizing that we were nuisances. Charles would tolerate a certain number of boyish pranks and then put his foot down, always without violence or recrimination. I knew what he knew, namely that he had recourse to Dad, and I seldom pushed him that far. Yet I was guided more by respect for my big brother than by fear, for he was right in just about everything. When he spoke, I listened. Still he joined in my idea of fun whenever appropriate—which was almost always. We worked well together in family chores, where Charles always did his share, and we even shared the same double bed where we kept each other warm on cold nights.

Charles, who had been carefully trained, as the first child should be in order to set an example, was discipline itself as the fine art of discipling. His level of leadership acknowledged me not only as a disciple, but as a colleague. I was never deprived of initiative, but privileged to learn from a gentle, consistent example. This also taught me that children as well as parents can joint venture this business of discipline. Charles had at least as moderating an effect on my rambunctious tendencies as did both of our parents. Although he was satisfied to be a skilled tradesman, it was he who unwittingly trained me as a professional leader.

However, this does not discount the example of our dad. An untiring worker, he set the pace for all of us. His sternness in old-fashioned honesty and his insistence on the work ethic were balanced by his tenderness with our mother and his ready hugs and affectionate words for each of us. This balance enabled him to bend the childish spirit without breaking it. Charles followed Dad more closely than I, but I was a disciple to both.

Some of the best known examples of discipleship range through the Torah, the Koran, and the Bible as Moses, Muhammad and Paul laid down godly principles and laws and lived the lives they preached. Yet the most notable of all examples was the Christ who taught discipling through the humblest of men—fishermen, tax gatherers, hangers-on—whom he turned into powerful forces for good.

So we see discipline as the sterling and exciting ethic of discipleship, whether as God to man, employer to employee, parent to child or child to child. Such discipling breeds a preparation in self-control that sparks parental leadership as consciously and unconsciously you teach by consistent example as well as by firm and congenial word. All through this book you will find example highlighted as the great teacher and consistency as its jewel.

Discipline is much broader than punishment. Discipline is an automobile; punishment is its brakes. Books and articles on discipline often concentrate on case studies in which we search for ways to make wrongs right. And such case studies offer one of the clearest ways to present a difficult and controversial subject. Yet, if we are going to turn delinquency trends around, we must do much more. Punishment should not be the main road to self-control.

No two behavior problems are exactly alike, so parents and teachers often find themselves somewhere in between the case studies, more frustrated than ever. Our approach here is to show early in this book how children grow and develop so that they have sound bases for judgment in discipline.

Few parents, even teachers, take time or spend effort to learn the developmental needs of children. So (1) they often make demands which their young cannot possibly meet, (2) they fail to set down consistent requirements which children of their ages can and should fulfill, and (3) they do not provide or allow for creative activities which may be different, yet appropriate for their ages. If you know how your youngsters develop and grow, you will know much better how to handle them.

All these may require adults to make some changes and learn to stress guidance more than reproof. For example, your youngsters at various ages may like water, mud, bugs, or even snakes, and they will surely like them at a time inconvenient to you. Yet these experiences open doors to curiosity and learning, which stimulate a creative mind that will one day make you proud. This was the making of Thomas Edison, Madame Curie, and George Washington Carver.

So discipline should be creative and seldom be punishment. Discipline can and should often be fun, while punishment is never enjoyable if we love our children. But discipline, lovingly viewed with commonsense and fascinatedly aware of how children learn and how they grow, can be the most intriguing of all family activities. You mold young lives just as the master sculptor shapes his clay, fires it, and brings out a vessel of beauty. You see children for what they really are—treasures to receive our closest scrutiny, support, and most tender care. You watch them grow—sometimes gradually, sometimes rapidly—in vision, awareness, reason, coordination, creativity, and eventually into maturity. You guide that growth with loving, firm awareness and consistency.

Your children must learn that you are in control from the moment of their birth. This is a process of *training,* much the same as you would prepare a puppy or a colt. There is not much *education* as such at first. They are only ready for educating as they become able to reason. Yet you will seek to become more and more aware of their potential to control themselves as day by day they flower before your very eyes. This transition from training to education takes place from birth to about age twelve.

Lessons from Pets

We do not suggest that pets are necessary. In fact, we sometimes insist that they may be a nuisance or even a hazard to your health. And certainly their care requires your patience and understanding and limits your freedom. Yet you and your children can learn much from training animals.

Oftentimes parents who are experienced in training animals tend to be more systematic and understanding in rearing their children. We have seen this in our son Dennis and the training of his big dog, Truckee, as well as his handling of children in and out of his classrooms. Just as he spent many hours teaching Truckee how to be "dead dog" or to ask "please" or to come at once, so he learned in schools in California, Colorado, and Michigan that many children require more than one admonition to learn a lesson. We have also seen it in the way our daughter Kathleen and her husband Bruce have reared both their big German shepherd and their three boys with the same formula of love, firmness, patient repetition, and consistency. Betty Cochran of the Hewitt-Moore Child Development Center, a former kennel owner, told the new owners of her kennel to think "two-legged" and always balance correction with love.

Whatever your religion, you are as God to your young, unreasoning infants. If you are demanding, unreasonable, uncontrolled, and harsh, they will think of God in that way. But if you love unconditionally, tenderly yet firmly, they will recognize God's wisdom in you. Remember, they need boundaries or they will not feel secure.

Children without set limits sense an aloneness in a very big world. If they do not learn to submit to you, it will be harder for them ever to submit to other authority, including to their God. You are not teaching them to submit to you as you would your dog, but to become *self*-controlled human beings, eventually to choose their own destinies. Your every response and example is their highest *training*.

As they become more and more "reason-able" you will operate less and less by fiat and more and more by choice. But you will maintain your rights to make final decisions until at least the teen years when they can accept the responsibility for the authority which your decisions imply.

Authority and responsibility must always be commensurate, always kept at the same level: Neither you nor the state dares to grant them the authority of driver's licenses until they can accept responsibility for driving. Throughout the period in which they are developing reason and responsibility, you grant them increasing power to choose their day-to-day activities. You insure that the choices you grant are those with which you can live.

The Nobility of Parenthood

The dignity or nobility you attach to your office as mother or father will depend to a great extent on whether you regard the future of your child as transient in this world or you look for an eternal world to come. We are not going to get distracted and argue religion here, for there are many kinds of beliefs and nearly all of them offer some kind of hope for the future. Yet in America it is particularly appropriate and defensible to make this reference because when we pledge our allegiance to our nation, we do it as "one nation under God." And wherever we go we carry in our billfolds and purses little slips of colored paper that say "In God We Trust."

We have in our custody offspring whose brains are so fabulously created that neurobiologists and computer experts together estimate that to do all the work possible by one normal human brain would require a computer so large that it would cover the entire earth—and still that device could not reason nor could it worship. Such a computer would only obey you as a robot.

To strengthen children's minds and to cultivate graces, to build strong bodies, and to develop loveliness of character are astonishing privileges. No king, prince, or other head of state has a more noble calling. In fact, as Leo Tolstoy tells it, the lowly shoemaker or minor shopkeeper is the greatest of all if his heart enfolds the widow and orphan.

And the greatest opportunity of all for creative neighborliness and the gift of self-sacrifice is the privilege in the home. It is the first court of law for the lawyer, the first chapel for the pastor, the first consulting room for the physician and the nurse, the first port for the ship's captain, the first place of building and repair for mechanic and carpenter, and the throne room for motherhood—the most noble profession of all.

Society cannot survive without the family. Greece went down when its parents gave their children to the state. That great nation was taken over by Rome, which in several centuries followed suit. And so dereliction has traveled through societies until today our nation is a tragic mirror of these earlier societies and one of the cultures more indifferent to family closeness.

Fathers and mothers are much more absorbed in their wants

and "freedoms" than they are with the needs of their children, not realizing that freedom without responsibility eventually means death. Children who have been trained by their peers instead of their parents will, after several generations of this indifference, have no standards, no strengths to pass on. And others will overtake them as surely as Rome conquered Greece. Here in America other institutions, especially schools, have tended to accommodate this parental lethargy rather than try to correct it. Ultimately, they have usurped more and more control and because of their natural limitations have encouraged these negative social developments. Our society is on a destruction course which can only be turned if parents demonstrate in word and action that they intend to retrieve control of their own.

Fathers are by historic design the heads of the family, the protectors of mothers and children. Whenever a society has turned from this patriarchal design, it has faded away. And the father must remember that responsibility must always move along commensurately with authority. While he may sometimes have to make a unilateral decision, he must remember that the woman he marries has equal share in respect, and he must be first to forgive, to be compassionate, and to protect his own. Without this warm kindness, in honor preferring others, the father will have only a house, never a home. But with that love, his woman will grant him great dignity—as any prince or king.

Mothers, on the other hand, have burdens few men understand. Making a home, caring for children in sickness and health, responding to cries, feeding husband and child, often uncertain of permanent residence or in financial distress, unable to walk away from trial, is a symphony of life that only a mother can fully understand. There is pain enough in childbirth and the fears that follow as little ones pass through the valley of the shadow, time and again.

While the mother normally has the larger responsibility in

care of her children, the father should mingle with them also whenever the opportunity affords. And he should see that this is frequent. He will take time to sympathize with his children in their little troubles, work *with* them in their little jobs, binding them to him with strong, but deep and tender, cords of love. The half hour or so the typical father spends weekly with his children should be multiplied at least ten or twenty times or more. And whenever possible the mother should be given a rest from the daily pressures and routines of modern home life.

These truths have come to me late in life. While I generally did spend mornings and evenings, and even noontimes, with my family in my home, I now realize that I presumed far too much on my wife. When she began to help me in our research and writing, I realized that she had to have some relief. Then I began preparing breakfast, making our bed, washing the dishes, cleaning the toilets, and doing my share of dusting, washing, cleaning, weed-pulling, and dozens of nuisance jobs. It was then I realized that authority and responsibility always go together and that the Golden Rule is a golden guide in the home.

The saying "The family that prays together stays together" is neither a trite phrase nor the property of any one religion. The father and mother who have a small realization of their responsibility to future generations will often come together in the family circle, whatever their religion. We have tried it. We know it works. We commend it to you. As you build and strengthen your values, material possessions will become less important than family in the building of your home. In your dignity and your nobility you will be among your nation's greatest citizens.

ᵥᵥᵥᵥᵥᵥᵥᵥᵥᵥᵥᵥᵥᵥᵥ 3 ᵥᵥᵥᵥᵥᵥᵥᵥᵥᵥᵥᵥᵥᵥᵥ
Comparative Discipline

If you are a person who likes questions, you might answer this one and be well on the road to creative discipline: If you have an expensive cherished car, camera, or stereo system that needs servicing, who would you seek to repair it—a general mechanic or one who is a factory-trained specialist for your specific make? In short, would you prefer a generalist or a specialist?

A good home is like the Rolls Royce factory. The specialist—the parent—knows his own product far better than the general mechanic who repairs all kinds of cars. Yet, there are also some similarities between the mass production factory and the place where autos are handmade. Both use tools; both use similar materials.

Most books on discipline relate to classroom control where the adult is responsible for a group of students from different home environments like the servicing of cars from many factories. But in the home, parents are specialists on the "products" of their own "factory"—producing, repairing, and restoring their own kind—in some respects a much simpler program with fewer risks and far greater promise of excellence than the remedial programs of social service agencies.

In a conventional classroom, the teacher's time, on the other hand, is preoccupied with many kinds of educational litter—reports, films, exercises—while trying to understand the individual differences of *many* children. The teacher is also trying to teach while reducing disruption in the classroom and

31

maintaining an atmosphere that brings good mental health and wholesome development.

But *how* the materials are used makes a great deal of difference in ultimate quality. For example, both parents and teachers should become acquainted with a variety of simple techniques and uncomplicated systems which apply to children wherever they are and which can prevent or remedy discipline problems. This includes first, the understanding of the way children develop and learn, and second, methods of dealing with discipline problems that are likely to arise. Both parents and teachers do well to:

1. Learn to think beyond punishment and control—beyond contingency systems for behavior—and become more involved in planning constructive and preventive programs that will bring out sound behavior.

2. Reflect upon and examine their own systems of belief in view of our times and their consistency in carrying them out—to strengthen not only their theories of discipline but also their practice of it.

Let's look at several widely published approaches to classroom discipline and see if they offer anything worthwhile for your home. Later we will steer a case study through these philosophies: Lee Canter's Assertive Discipline, Rudolf Dreikurs' Logical Consequences, and Thomas Gordon's Teacher Effectiveness Training—a takeoff on his P-E-T (Parent Effectiveness Training). After that, we will take the best of so-called modern techniques and combine them with an understanding of how children develop and learn. This is the key to happy rearing of children. And we emphasize here again the importance of your view of discipline. It should be considered a genuinely creative opportunity. As in any creative process there will be times when you have to reconsider and start over again, but properly viewed, the process should be exciting and for the most part happy.

Assertive Discipline

Canter recommends that teachers take charge decisively in the classroom, firmly communicating their wants and needs to their students and demonstrating that they are prepared to enforce their words with action. He advocates teacher power without apology and stresses the teachers' rights:

1. The right to establish a classroom structure and routine that provides the best learning environment *considering the teacher's own strengths and weaknesses.*

2. The right to determine and demand appropriate behavior from students, which meets the teacher's needs and encourages positive social and educational development in the students.

3. The right to require help from parents, the principal, etc., when the teacher needs assistance with a child.[1]

Unfortunately, Canter doesn't seem much concerned about the teacher's need to understand the *causes* of children's misbehavior in order to deal effectively with them. In fact, he feels that such attitudes often contribute to the problem of classroom disruption because they make teachers feel that certain children can't be expected to behave properly since they are victims of unfortunate circumstances beyond their control.

Dr. Canter is a confronter, a unilateral authoritarian. And there is something to say for this approach, especially during the years before adolescence, and also in the military. Indeed most children have a particular understanding of how much they can get by with and will abide by the limits if they are clearly set down and consistently enforced. He suggests that teachers (1) establish few rules, (2) state them clearly to the students, (3) enforce them consistently, and (4) make clear the consequences in the event rules are violated. He insists that a succession of progressively more severe measures should be laid down for each additional rule infraction.

Canter also tells teachers to explain their discipline plans to parents and to insist on their support. And they are to make clear their plans to their superiors so that they have the support of the school administration.

He advocates systematic, relentless punishment for misbehavior and recommends that teachers offer abundant positive rewards for good behavior. And he prescribes that quality of regular communication with parents which emphasizes the positive accomplishments of their children.

Logical Consequences

On the other hand, Rudolph Dreikurs outlines an approach to discipline that suggests identifying and dealing with the *causes* of misbehavior in his book, *Discipline Without Tears*. "All behavior is purposive," Dreikurs says. "You can't understand the behavior of another person unless you know what he is trying to accomplish." And, broadly speaking, Dreikurs says that "the youngster is always trying to develop some kind of identity. So if a person or child misbehaves he has wrong ideas about how to be significant."

Dr. Dreikurs contends that there are four types of motives which underlie the misbehavior of children: (1) the need for attention; (2) the need to exercise power; (3) the motive of revenge; and (4) the motive to protect themselves through displays of helplessness and inadequacy. He suggests that confronting the child with direct questions about the probable cause of his misbehavior will help in diagnosing the problem.

For the child who genuinely needs attention, Dreikurs recommends that he be given such attention when his behavior merits it. But when he seeks attention through misbehavior, he should be ignored.

Dreikurs is an avoider, a compromiser. For the child who wants to exert power over you, he recommends that you stay out of the power struggle. Do not demonstrate how powerless the child is compared with you. Neither should you allow him to dominate you. Show respect for the child and try to reach an agreement in which no one loses. Punish misbehavior by imposing logical consequences which reflect the realities of social life and not your personal need to dominate the child. Recognize the child's legitimate need to feel powerful within the limits of his maturity and give him opportunities to use power productively.

For the child who seeks revenge, Dreikurs recommends that you react as one who has been hurt rather than assuming a vengeful attitude or retaliating. Use logical consequences as punishment, but emphasize those qualities in the child that are good. For children who display helplessness and inadequacy in an effort to protect themselves, Dreikurs recommends encouragement more than control, and he stresses group discussion.[2] He does not seem to recognize that children may need consistent, firm, and loving direction.

Teacher Effectiveness Training

Thomas Gordon's methods are designed to improve student behavior without resorting to adult power and authority. He encourages a positive student-teacher relationship, which fosters directness and honesty and increases willingness to take risks in reaching understandings. He wants teachers and students to care conspicuously for one another. Yet he believes in independence for both parties, minimizing the student's dependency on adults. Gordon stresses the individuality of both parties and the mutual meeting of needs, with neither party meeting his or her needs at the expense of the other.

Gordon asks the question: Who owns the problem? If it is the student's problem, the teacher can be most helpful by listening empathetically and helping the student to clarify his or her own feelings and formulate an approach to the solution.[3]

Gordon feels that students' words are often uniquely coded

messages that are not always clearly understood in relation to the feelings that prompt them. He believes that they must be decoded, getting at the underlying sentiment being expressed and "feeding" it back to the student. Like Carl Rogers' "nondirective counseling," he would have you actively listen, ask occasional questions, but give little direct counsel and demonstrate virtually no authority.

Gordon lists a number of roadblocks to communication: constant warning, ordering, generalizing, blaming, and judging. In his view, these tend to close down the open expression of feeling. If you have a problem involving a child, the idea is to communicate your feelings directly to your student or child. Focus on *your* needs and how they are affected by the student's actions. Gordon calls these "I-messages" because they emphasize how I (the sender of the message) am affected instead of you (the student receiving the message). An I-message has three elements:

1. It identifies and clearly states what is causing the problem—the specific student behavior involved.

2. It makes clear the tangible effect which this has on you, the teacher or parent-teacher.

3. It conveys in tone or words how you, the teacher, feel about the situation.

Gordon feels that this approach has the highest probability of promoting a *willingness* on the part of the student to change and is least apt to injure the relationship, which he sees as a most powerful means of influencing positive behavior.

Gordon's approach concerns us because the "I-messages" seldom insure control. Without firm consistency of precept and example, many children will not be impressed. Gordon doesn't go as far as A. S. Neill in his descriptions of *Summerhill,* which are pictures of almost total child license, yet he largely lacks the firmness and consistency that Canter tends to overdo. We feel that Canter's firmness and consistency is effective only when it grows out of love and an understanding of how children develop and learn.

First, let's take a case mostly involving school and weave through the ideas of Canter, Dreikurs and Gordon with the help of some child psychologist friends, bearing in mind that no two professionals agree on precisely what these so-called authorities are trying to say. No one system is perfect, so perhaps we can learn from each of them. Also, much depends on your personality and commitment to your children. Second, we will consider a home case. And finally we will close these comparisons with the developmental approach of this book—how children become ready as they grow older—or what you might call here the "Moore approach."

The Case of Doug Owens

Doug Owens was thirteen, the second of three children, and the only boy. His father had been killed by accident while on active duty in the U.S. Army in North Korea. His mother sustained her little family on a small pension and the few dollars she and the children made on the side. Because of the neighborhood in which they lived, Doug was forced to associate with low-income youngsters who were well salted with delinquency. While he was a leader among them and vulnerable to peer pressures, he still had ideals ingrained by his father whose memory he held dear.

Doug was a typically curious boy who had experimented occasionally with cigarettes, yet he had turned from them in large part because of his father's wise and solemn counsel through the years. This had also kept him away from alcohol and drugs, for his father neither smoked nor drank.

Doug was still careful about girls, not only because of the example of his dad, but because he was the "man" of the family and had an affectionately happy relationship with his mother and sisters—whom he called "my special women." Yet out of boredom and reaction to a rigid, effeminate male teacher he became something of a nuisance at school. Too often he pulled pranks—like setting off an alarm clock, timed for a visit from his teacher's supervisor, and tossing a small firecracker into the girls' restroom. His mother sometimes was in tears, but more because of fear of the teacher than of Doug's basic behavior; she was certain he would get over it and thought his teacher was "an angry man."

Mr. Remington, his teacher, demanded that the kids kowtow—to use their mildest term. Yet he did not get their respect. The bolder of the youngsters described Mr. R. as "a homo," "a sissy," or "not fair."

Canter's Approach

First, let's see how Remington would have handled Doug as a dyed-in-the-wool disciple of Dr. Canter. Remington was handicapped, particularly with the boys, in trying to carry out a rigid Canter program of order. Confrontation was his favorite ploy. This should have pleased Canter, except that the teacher picked on Doug, according to some of the boys, because Doug wouldn't talk back to him. This was not according to Canter's hopeful plan.

So Remington kept Doug in at recess and said, "Doug, you're in deep trouble for throwing that firecracker into the girls' restroom this morning. I have a notion to turn you over to the police. When are you going to grow up? Don't you know that's against the law?"

"No, I didn't think . . ."

Though rebellion built inside of him, Doug indeed did not want to get mixed up with the law, and he thought about its possible implications on his mother and sisters. So he satisfied (temporarily, at least) Remington's goals when he answered, in accordance with his home training, "I'm sorry, sir. I won't do it again."

"Okay," Remington replied, "but you're going to have to

give me all the firecrackers you have left, and you'll be marked down this quarter in deportment. And I'm grounding you from sports for a week." (Can you think of better punishments?)

Although sometimes Doug had been guilty, his teacher's futile confrontations accused him of many things he had not in fact done. Principal Adams knew this, but Remington thought the principal was partial and too protective of Doug. Although Mr. Adams was well known for his understanding ways, there may have been something to the partiality idea, for Mr. Adams had known Doug's father as a close friend and had more than a little sympathy for the boy. He was trying to hold things steady until the end of the school year when Doug would be "out from under" the unfriendly teacher.

Canter's confrontation technique appears useful primarily to teachers who have the respect of their students and their parents. And it can only succeed, if at all, when a genuine effort is made by school staffs to understand the student and his background, with a determination to build him into a valued and productive citizen. Yet this does not appear to be Canter's primary emphasis nor that of Mr. Remington, who as a confronter was almost hopelessly handicapped in this case because of his femininity.

Dreikurs' Philosophy

Now let's consider Mr. Remington as if he were a Dreikurs fan. Instead of confronting Doug with an accusation, he assumed a vengeful motive on Doug's part and acted hurt. He called Doug in and said, "I'm disappointed in your throwing a firecracker into the girls' restroom this morning. What do you have against me or the girls?"

Because Mr. R. was not a respected "male" model, neither Doug nor any of the boys tended to be sympathetic with him, so Doug shrugged his shoulders and said, "Nothing." Even to the question, "Why did you do it?" Doug simply dug his toe into the floor and said he didn't know. And when Mr. R. said,

"What do you think is a reasonable consequence?" Doug's response was just the same.

Under the circumstances the teacher was not gaining much ground, as far as present discipline or future behavior is concerned. He was furious down inside from the futility of dealing with the boy.

"Doug." He finally gestured with his hand extended, palm up. "Do you have any more firecrackers?"

"Yeah."

"Give me the rest of the firecrackers. This may help you avoid such trouble again."

Because Doug's training restrained him from back talk or direct confrontation, he reluctantly handed some of his firecrackers to Mr. Remington.

Probably Mr. R.'s chief weakness in this method, other than his basic personality, was that he did not take the time to study the needs of his students. He also had so little use for kindness and justice that he was adamant against reasoning by his principal, muttering to other teachers something about wanting "to dethrone him." He passed the word that Doug was "impossible." And Mr. R. was furious when he found out that Mr. Adams was working closely with Doug's family, even having Doug and his mother and sisters over for dinner.

Mr. Adams was confident of the basic family integrity and their loyalty to the memory and ideals of their late husband and father. He saw no reason to compromise or to avoid truth "when you have people like Doug and his family who are honest to the last gnat's whisker."

Gordon's Likely Solution

Now let's try to put Mr. Remington into Gordon's soup kettle, which at first sip is more tasty than Canter's and more consistent than Dreikurs'. He would not have had the right to exercise the authority he now was misusing. And we argue here that authority is needed by all families and schools to the extent that they are held responsible for those in their care. Gordon does not seem to acknowledge this authority-responsibility equation which we insist must always be commensurate. And this goes both ways—for adults and for children. For example, you don't let a child use matches until he is responsible, and when he *does* arrive at that maturity level, it is your obligation to honor his responsibility with appropriate authority.

Remington feebly attempted the carrot and stick idea, but used it more as a bribe than as an inducement, and the boys didn't "buy it." His method with the firecracker episode went like this:

"I am very disappointed by your throwing a firecracker into the girls' restroom this morning, Doug. I am especially concerned about the possible danger involved and also the stress it puts on the girls. You know, of course, that it is also against the law."

Because of the last sentence, Doug was jarred to respond somewhat cooperatively and replied, "I'm sorry, sir, I won't do it again."

However, there was no real understanding in the process, either of Doug or of the offense, mostly because of teacher time and attention limitations. A teacher (or parent) has to give a great deal in order to know and care for each student, and relatively few have the commitment to do this thoroughly. The immediate symptoms are treated, as simply and as effectively as putting a Band-Aid on a cancer. The cause is seldom determined; the real disease, ignored.

Doug obviously needed a strong hand to guide him. His father had been a genuine authority figure; but his had been a gloved fist—firm and consistent with principle, while remaining gentle and kind.

Gordon offers part of the answer, particularly with children from age ten and above who are able to reason, analyze, and understand logical consequences. In addition, adults who strive to be good disciplinarians must realize that the problem may be theirs as much as their children's, whereas Gordon seems to assume that the problem is usually the student's (or the child's).

We believe it wise to observe here that for classroom success in discipline it is more important for a teacher to understand children and to know parents than to be certified, assuming reasonable competency in subject matter or an ability to help children find the answers. When Dorothy was a beginning teacher and later a reading specialist with the Whittier, California, schools, her superintendent required that every one of his teachers visit the home of each student before the school year started to talk with the parents and if possible, have a little chat with the child involved. Dorothy did this and found it very effective. As district superintendent in Artesia, California, I required it of all teachers and paid them for the extra time and travel required. This was not unusual in those days, and the students' behavior usually reflected this effort.

If Remington had been a mature, balanced teacher exuding a male image and had shown even casual understanding and appreciation of Doug's background and circumstances, he could have built Doug into a thoroughly positive leader. As it was, Mr. Adams worked with Doug during the summer from a developmental approach, bearing in mind six factors:

1. Doug was buoyant, active, not depressed. He was creative and idealistic, yet he required firm guidance in his early teens, for without a strong father to influence him most of the time, he already revealed a tendency to knuckle under to peer pressures. His leadership capacity needed the challenge which his ideals could support. This, Mr. Adams intended to do, discreetly reminding Doug of his privilege and responsibility to his classmates, his family, and his father's memory—in contrast to the rather silly pranks which had often occupied him.

2. Doug was vulnerable to an appeal to principle. He knew his dad as that kind of man. This idealism provided great leverage for the principal (who was also a principled man).

3. The dinner invitation got Mr. Adams off to a good start. If someone had done something similar much earlier, perhaps utilizing the help of other neighbors, much pain could have been avoided. Oftentimes parents can make better progress with their own children by discreetly asking the friendship or help of friends whom their errant or questioning children consider worthy of confidence and unbiased.

4. We happened to be one of the neighbors, and when his need was mentioned to us, we lost no time in reminding Doug how much he was like his dad—basically honest and strong.

5. We nevertheless talked firmly with him (as arranged with Mr. Adams), analyzing his situation, his reactions to his teacher, his conduct and his potential, including his male leadership in his family, and how he could make the most of it as unto his father and his God.

6. Working with Mr. Adams, and obtaining some concessions in terms of school time, we helped Doug get started in business cleaning up yards, selling junk, helping start gardens, and doing odd jobs and even some baby sitting. His sisters joined him in many of his activities, with his mother guiding him as chairman of his company. He was president, his sisters, ages eleven and nine, were vice president and secretary, and a number of his classmates worked as his employees and commission agents. The last we heard, he was preparing to make a bid on an old house which he hoped to fix up and sell at age fifteen—eventually to get enough money to buy his mother a new car.

Solution of Doug's problem would have been more likely if the teacher had been understanding of children and had taken time and effort to study the family history and the boy's needs and potential. But he was "too busy" and otherwise disinclined "to do a total biographical investigation of the kid." Moreover, Doug was in need of a male authority figure to take the place of his father.

Although much more friendly than Canter's and less fickle than Dreikurs', Gordon's philosophy does not provide for authority as needed by all families and all schools. It does not insist that such power—for the child or parent or teacher—be commensurate with each person's responsibility. Its indulgent, expedient approach does not grasp the reality and complexity of Doug's situation.

Turning Children Around

Let's take the case of ten-year-old Rick, who had a problem at home. He was the mischief scourge of the neighborhood. His father had deserted the family of one boy and two girls of whom Rick was the oldest. In his little California town the economy was flat during the period when gasoline prices skyrocketed, and motor home and camper manufacturers went bankrupt. His mother was on Aid to Dependent Children (ADC) and bought most of her groceries with food stamps. But the family was generally clean and honest—qualities that greatly help build a program of good child behavior.

Ricky's pastor understood his needs and set out to help him toward higher goals than being the village nuisance as a graffiti specialist and trickster. He invited Rick to help in his vegetable garden for a few dimes a day. The boy was both delighted to be able to work with a man and fascinated to watch the plants grow.

Before long he was asking his mother to start a garden of their own, and when she hesitated, he told her, "I will teach you how." His self-worth was already building. At first he made only a few cents a day, but his mother and sisters delighted in dining on "the stuff from our very own garden." Before the summer was out Rick was selling over twenty dollars daily of produce from his garden, with the help of his mother and sisters. When his garden began to run down, he kept up his vegetable route by buying from the local wholesale cooperative. And he no longer had time to get into mischief. This was done with a minimum of confrontation, much personal *adult* friendship, and an understanding of his needs.

A Change in Cory

Still another case which illustrates both problems at home and at school is that of a ten-year-old girl. Cory lived in the same town as Rick and was a bad influence on him. She was down on everything, not only because of the down economy, but also because of the indifference of her mother who came home from work too tired to care. Cory's dad was basically a good man, but not very energetic, and because he was unable to get work, he was always "in Cory's hair."

It did not help any that she was an early maturing child who had begun her monthly periods and whose father somehow did not understand, in the words of her mother, that "there are times when girls are just not themselves." Cory began to run around with an older girl of doubtful reputation in her church and two others from a nearby public school who had been her classmates the year before. Cory's school record—mostly D's and F's, with an occasional C—belied her very bright mind. She was almost constantly complaining about her teacher and her principal as "sick."

In an effort to offset peer influences and place her in a better environment, her parents enrolled her in a Christian school which had recently started a work-study program in which students could work most, if not all, of their way through school. Supervised by teachers and a layman or two who also worked with them, the elementary school students worked well, from grades one through eight—except for Cory who was grumpy, largely because of the putdowns of her three girl friends who said the work program was "cruddy."

And then the principal stepped in. Without confrontation or

any sad pleas, he assessed Cory for what she was: a ten-year-old who was physically mature beyond her years, but had a poor sense of self-worth. Although she was only a fourth grader, he knew she was sharp enough, and her mother had trained her to be careful enough that he assigned her as "quality control officer" on the assembly line that made wooden toys and "packages" for shipping honeybees. She responded like a champion and became the best they had ever had on quality control. Within days her studies improved, and by the end of the semester she was getting all A's and B's. And her fascination with her agemates faded as she became more involved in improving herself and making her school projects a success.

WHAT IF? If you were to ask Cory about her present teacher or her principal, you would receive a delighted answer. But where would she be if Mr. Remington had been her teacher? If she had been confronted à la Canter? If her teacher and principal had avoided or compromised with her inclinations, per Dreikurs? Or yet if they had followed Gordon's suggestions and waited her out with nondirective counseling?

Applying the Six Hints

Her principal and teacher either deliberately or instinctively made use of the six hints above: (1) They understood Cory's developmental needs, as an early pubescent girl from an unhappy economic family situation and with doubtful peer association, and set out deliberately to meet them, including a careful assessment of how much authority and responsibility she could handle. (2) They were concerned with a much higher level of response than simple punishment or reward normally bring. (3) They became significant people in her life in a positive way, providing her strong models for her own self-worth as they worked with her and the other students. (4) They made clear what they expected. (5) They themselves were secure in their program, operating on principle so as to know exactly where they were going, providing a powerful

sense of security to all. (6) Their program was genuinely creative as with enthusiasm they combined the proven recipe of
balancing head, heart, hand, and health.

Dorothy summarizes this process in her unique way. A remedial method which worked best for her was always to deal
with a child at the *first* infraction, not in punishment but in a
challenge which fit the child's maturity. For example, she
would appeal to a boy's opportunity as an athlete or work
leader or to a specific talent—in music, art, leadership—as a
model for others. Her goal was always to show confidence by
giving a child a special job or responsibility which challenged
him, even at some risk for her! Sometimes she had to devise a
task that was not really necessary, yet she always tried to fix
young eyes on higher goals, keeping the students on the
stretch instead of indulging them.

Ultimately you will develop your own system of discipline.
You will have your own style. As any skilled potter forms the
clay into a graceful vessel, you will study your "material" and
bring out noble creations. We will try to help you understand
that material in the chapters that follow through an understanding of how children develop—what can be expected at
various ages and stages of growth. And then we will offer a
few practical, proven recipes for commonsense discipline.

Selecting the Best from Authorities (The Moore Approach)

We believe that the ultimate test of effective discipline is to
determine whether or not it has become part of your children's
nature, whether students have developed some inner system
of initiative and self-restraints (self-control), which cause them
to act in ways appropriate to their own highest and most selfless interests and the interests of others.

To do this best, your goal will be to *act* in a deliberate way
rather than to *react* defensively, as you try to build self-control
in yourself and your children or students. Here are some hints:

1. Plan carefully in terms of the maturity of your children and the unique characteristics of each. We stress in this book the crucial need to understand how children develop generally and that they may greatly differ individually. Some are quiet types; others, buoyant. Some ponder; others are quick to act. And so on and on. But *you* are in control, and *you* only release that control as your youngsters are able to accept the authority which assumes equivalent responsibility. As your students become more and more consistently reasonable, you can trust them with heavier decisions. This will require an understanding of children, and we try in this book to help you meet that need.

2. While they are not necessarily bad, remember that simple punishment and reward tend to stimulate lower levels of moral development. Understanding of and commitment to principle permit students to move to higher levels of morality.[4]

3. Higher levels are developed by building a genuine sense of self-worth. Such students are definitely less inclined to behave in undesirable ways. This is like looking in a mirror. Children tend to see themselves largely in terms of the way they are viewed and treated by the significant people in their lives. If their parents and peers expect more constructive behavior, children will more likely live up to their expectations. But peers seldom provide strong models. If the youngsters can be with their parents more and if parents are alert and thoughtful to their needs, the chances are the children will be better behaved.[5]

4. Teacher (or parent) expectation has a powerful influence on student behavior. It is most effective when it functions in the range of challenge, where success seems quite possible but not certain or automatic, not without effort. Your expectation is generally best expressed by example—patience, strength, optimism, integrity.

5. When children admire their teachers, parents, and other relatives and friends and desire to please them, disci-

pline problems fall dramatically. But don't let this knowledge lead you to the inconsistent softness of indulgence. You should operate only on the basis of principle—always having a sound reason for your actions. As a first step in building rapport, you should make a deliberate effort to understand yourself.[6]

6. There are, of course, a variety of other factors which promote creative discipline: (a) optimism and humor, (b) novel experience, (c) teacher enthusiasm, (d) reasonably careful planning and organization, (e) group identity and *esprit de corps* in family or classroom—the idea of being on a team.

PART TWO

DISCIPLINE THROUGH UNDERSTANDING

Prevention: Control through Knowing

While we were living in Japan, an American family came over one day for counsel about a problem more common than most parents realize: their four-year-old neighbor, a son of American missionaries, had invited their three-year-old daughter over to "play house." None of the parents knew of the goings on until little Debbie told her mother that "it hurts down here." Further questioning revealed that the boy had been fondling "my toidy" with "his dirty hands," and had been showing her "his thing." The parents eventually discovered that the boy had been doing this with others in the compound for over a year. Some of the offended parents had not said anything because the father of the boy was the head of the mission there; so they simply did not allow their children to play with the boy except under strict supervision.

This reluctance to deal with the matter directly was of course unfair to the little boy, who should have been dealt with gently, promptly, and firmly. His father assured the offended family that he and his wife had repeatedly "explained why this was a no-no." They were mystified that their boy was "being nasty" again. What they had not understood was that at age three or four children are not able to reason consistently enough to fully understand such explanations. What the young boy *did* require at his age was a parental fiat: "NO! NEVER!" and a daily check on his activities until they were certain they had made their point.

On the other hand, as children grow older we must deal with matters more and more from reason, until eventually they leave us, self-disciplined and responsibly on their own. Meanwhile we can only discipline effectively as we understand how they develop—in senses, reasoning, brain development, coordination, and assimilation of values.

When we look back on how little we knew when we had our own children, we are appalled. We were supposed to be well trained professionals, yet we knew almost nothing of practical value. We knew little about preventing misbehavior. Fortunately, we were given a good book—now long out of print—written by a woman pediatrician who had five children of her own. It was a lifesaver for us and the source of our success in child rearing. We have echoed many of its principles in our book *Home Grown Kids,* which will give you many additional hints on how to enjoy your children from birth instead of viewing childrearing as a battle and a long, hard march.

Many of us parents know less about how children develop than we know about how our cars run. And that is not very much. How would you score, for instance, on a quiz that asks how gasoline makes power or how the motor is connected to the wheels? Many parents make decisions about their children with as little understanding. Why do we let an infant decide when he should eat and sleep when we wouldn't think of letting a two-, three-, or even six-year-old make that choice? Or why do we give our children sugared snacks when they come home from school?[1]

The care and feeding and discipline of our young children today is about as planned as Russian roulette. Most of us are peer dependent in our practices, largely following the dictates of advertising men and our neighbors without asking why. And our children suffer; some even die. Few parents fully use their animal instincts to rear their young, a profession that deserves the highest powers of reason. Mice will choose whole-grained foods over the refined items we hand to our children. In simplest words, love and thoughtfulness are our greatest tools. Thoughtfulness asks principled questions—What are the basic reasons for standard practices today?—and evaluates common practices rather than blindly adopting them.

Many years ago in San Pablo, California, my brother and I begged our father for some little chickens like the ones kids had up the road. Our mother had died, and Grandma Moore was caring for us while Dad was at work. Dad decided to combine child rearing and chicken raising; he would experiment with our training as we learned about our feathered friends. He wanted us to see the whole life cycle, from birth to death, so he planned to start with one rooster and at least two hens. Besides, in those days we did not have automatic incubators and brooders to hatch the eggs and keep the little chickens warm.

He questioned us closely to see what we had learned from the neighbors so that he knew how much we already understood. Then he made us pledge to care for our chickens every day.

I remember well the excitement in our home the day he brought home a big Rhode Island Red rooster and two beautiful hens, one for my brother and one for me. Under his tender direction, we learned how to take care of chickens. He took our pledge that we would tend them every day. I will never forget how I failed one night to see that the chickens were in the pen and lost a hen to a skunk.

Dad knew chickens—and us—and when to punish and not to punish five- and seven-year-old boys. He found another hen. Then we had to find how to persuade a live hen to accept the dead hen's eggs, which were almost ready to hatch. We learned to raise chickens—how to feed them, clean their pens, let them out into the grass, nest them, and keep them from pecking each other.

Chickens provide a quick and clear analogy of human development: fertilization of the egg; warmth and tender care of the eggs by the mother hen or incubator; and the hatching of

55

little chicks. Then comes the work of feeding the babies, cleaning their leavings and getting new straw for their bedding, controlling their behavior, and protecting them from all surrounding threats. Unfortunately many parents fail to give the informed attention to their children that they give to their pets.

Nearly all discipline problems in one way or another originate from a lack of understanding of the way children "tick." Child development is not an exact science. When researchers tell you there will likely be growth spurts at ages four to six, eight to ten, and twelve to fourteen, bear in mind that those are average ages. Don't be surprised if they are five to seven, nine to eleven, and thirteen to fifteen or earlier or later. Yet some knowledge of children's developmental *trends* can make life much easier for both you and them.

Although nearly all parents dislike trouble of any kind, few have willingly learned how to avoid it or to "fix it." And trouble can be of different dimensions. For example, we will find as we pound away in this book that we have *instant trouble* if we try to operate a computer without some understanding of its programs. Likewise, you will have *night and day trouble* if you don't have an idea of how to meet your baby's needs.[2] And you will go through endless trouble and agony for the rest of your life if you try to discipline without some understanding of how your children develop in the four H's—head, hand, heart, and health—and in the social packaging of all four.

If you assume that your children will grasp the logic of your instructions and your actions before they have developed enough to be able to reason consistently, you may burn out, and in turn, they will become frustrated with you. If you expect all of your children to develop at about the same rate in the same abilities, you are asking for frustration, anxiety, and big disappointments.

We present here a simple, up-to-date consensus on how children actually develop and, in a small way, how their development applies directly or indirectly to their discipline.[3] Some of these developmental needs, all well established, will almost surely cut across your child-rearing practices if you are at all conventional. Yet if you are brave enough to experiment with them, the chances are you will actually enjoy a creative experience in discipline because your children will be far less trouble.

▪▪▪▪▪▪▪▪▪▪▪▪▪▪▪▪ 5 ▪▪▪▪▪▪▪▪▪▪▪▪▪▪▪▪

Dealing with Tantrums

Occasionally there arises a case study which seems desperate and which involves an unusually wide range of opportunities for action. Recently such a case emerged in a long, handwritten letter Dorothy and I received from a frantic mother of an infant boy, age eighteen months, whom she and her husband adopted while they were on a trip overseas. The little fellow "has a terrible temper" and what she characterizes as "a mean streak." He likes to scream and shout, bites, kicks, and slaps anyone around. He throws his bottle, dinner plate, or whatever he happens to have in his hands at anyone who comes near him.

She has been patient, but in the last six months her patience "has been wearing thin." She has tried spanking, without success, and now fears that his mean streak may be getting to her—bringing out anger in her that she didn't know before existed. She is afraid of losing her temper: "He seems to have picked up on that, and now he knows what buttons to push to send me over the edge, and he does it occasionally in what seems to be a very deliberate attempt to rouse my anger." Yet she assures us, "I love him very much."

Specialists believe that he is "very bright." His language ability is not up with his motor ability, so "he is frustrated because he cannot communicate." A more rigid program has been suggested. A physician's wife thought he might well be separated from her more of the time, perhaps in day care or at least nursery school by age three. But the mother has read our books on children and early schooling and hesitates. It is good that she does. Here is the letter that Dorothy wrote her, which supplies many answers for many problems in one communication, and I believe is worthy of this book, for what you may use with your children or students. Please bear in mind that this was a mother, but the principles and basic methods are universal.

Dear Mrs. Doran,

You have given us a large order, especially since I know so little about you or your little boy. But when a child only eighteen months old is so out of control as you indicate, you surely will need to do something promptly. Normally I would need to ask you a lot of questions, but in lieu of that, I will make some general suggestions which have worked for me and others. God will help you turn this situation around.

In any case remedial methods will be much more painful and severe for both you and David than constructive and preventive would have been. Though you are obviously loving and committed, I suspect that you are not really firm and consistent, and the little one has taken advantage of you. A mere infant is perfectly capable of doing this—not because he is cognitively mature enough to reason things out, but because it is natural for him to be ego-centered and to demand immediate gratification.

I assume some indulgence on your part, because of the response of the doctor's wife who felt that David needed to be away from you more—an indication that she considers you incapable of controlling him. She evidently concluded that his will was dominant when he should be submissive to your will—*at least in the first few years before he is able to reason*. You must not give up now, because if he does not submit to your will, he will not be able to submit to any authority, including God's. Actually such behavior is making him just as miserable as you.

Children have varied temperaments and some are

59

obviously more difficult to handle than others, but I am a firm believer in the influence of training and environment, to a much greater extent than heredity. I believe that both inherited and cultivated tendencies to evil can be changed. Since your techniques have not worked, you are going to have to take an entirely different tack. *You are the one who is going to have to change first.*

In general you should calmly say what you mean, move with consideration, and carry out what you say without deviation. You show your love best by being firm, decisive, and positive in your dealings with him. Remember that God also means what He says, and though He is a God of love and forgiveness when we are repentant, consequences most assuredly follow actions in this life. We reap what we sow. Consider these suggestions carefully:

1. Did you carefully control David's routine from the time he came under your care or did he decide when he should eat, sleep, play or have a bath? The current popular method is to cater to the baby's every whim, allowing the infant to be in control. This is the permissive way which has and is bringing on a most undisciplined generation. If you did not carefully control the routine, you missed the first and most important step in discipline. He had you "psyched out" early on and has taken advantage of you ever since. This routine should have been his rules of conduct in action, though not in word. Your loving but decisive tone of voice and handling of him in every part of his program should convey the fact that you are in charge.

If he is not on a systematic program at this time, you should immediately institute a regular mealtime, nap time, bedtime, bath time and play time—as regular as the clock. If he fusses or causes any problem at mealtime, he must not be allowed to eat, nor to disturb your eating. He should leave the table and go to his room without *anything* to eat until the next meal, except water, no matter how he might cry, plead, or scream. I have known of children greatly improving with just this simple technique. Such routine promotes physical, mental, and emotional well-being, for it keeps the natural body rhythms in synchronization and the child knows what to expect. Remember that young children are creatures of routine—in which they feel secure. An undisciplined child very often has problems learning.

I assume that some of his meals are not with the family. If he is difficult at mealtime, it may be that until his behavior changes, all his meals should be by himself—a regular early supper, for example, and then to bed early. I would suggest that his vegetable meal be at noon and then just a fresh fruit and toast meal for supper. I assume he is on three meals a day.

How is David's diet? Is there any reason to suspect allergies or sensitivity to sugar? There is a *very close* connection between diet and behavior. I would take David *completely* off of sugar and honey at least for a while. Substitute fruit. That can't hurt anything and may help a great deal. Milk, cheese, and chocolate are other "suspect" foods.

2. Remember that David understands very well what you tell him and has understood since he was 7 or 8 months old, knowing to what extent he would be indulged. So you should tell him kindly and firmly that the next time he has a tantrum, screams, or demonstrates any other violent behavior he will be sent to his room alone until he comes smiling to you and is sorry. You should tell him that you love him very much but that his crying hurts your ears and that you will no longer stand for his naughtiness.

Then, if and when the event occurs, keep your word. When he is repentant, he should make a commitment about future actions. Only then should he be allowed to come back into the family area and be accepted. Tell him that such behavior makes both you and him unhappy, but express confidence that he will not do it again. Many parents seal the event by kneeling together and praying for help to be a loving, kind, obedient child. Perhaps have him repeat a simple sentence or two after you in prayer also.

If his tantrum occurs in a place where you cannot remove him, there are other things you could do. One time when our son turned red and blue in a tantrum, I happened to have a pitcher of ice water within reach, which I threw right in my son's face—it even surprised me, but he never did it again. You and whoever is there might just leave the room or otherwise isolate him, for there is no point in his tantrum if there is no audience. You must *never* give him his way with such behavior. The more times he misbehaves the harder it is to cure him, because his will is strengthened each time by his victory.

3. In some cases you might find that an inducement will work. I am not speaking of bribes or material gifts, but if you are thinking of some little thing David likes very much to do—go to the playground at the park or some such thing— tell him that down at the park they like happy boys, so if he does not cry or scream once all day, you and he will go— after his nap. Then, of course, be prepared to stay home if misbehavior should occur. You must always do exactly what you say you are going to do. Consistency is a jewel of jewels in discipline.

4. There is nothing wrong with an occasional spanking, but of course it should never be done in anger nor for the gratification of the parent—only for the child's good. It is usually best done with a switch of some kind—which stings but does not injure—on the legs or bare bottom. Yet it is not usually the best treatment for a tantrum, screaming or violent temper, because such behavior is uncontrolled anger and *spanking is of no value until the child has calmed down and you can deal with him calmly*. Then, he may no longer need a spanking, for he knows very well that he has been naughty.

When a spanking is indicated in the case of a direct, presumptuous violation of your request, he should be gently, even lovingly and plainly told that this is to "help him remember," or "help him learn to obey." He should clearly know why he was spanked and in most cases be able to tell you ahead of time what he did that was unacceptable. If either of you is angry, the spanking should be delayed until you both have cooled down. Then, if he is duly repentant, the spanking may not be needed. Nearly everyone becomes angry occasionally. It is what you do about it that makes the difference.

5. It may be that David has been able to get what he wanted by crying or whining, and this violent crying has simply been an outgrowth of that. The rule really should be that you *give nothing for which the child cries*. It is easy to get into the habit of "answering" his needs (which are usually *wants*) in this way and to be largely controlled by his cries, especially in his early weeks and months. It is better to anticipate needs and wants, and offer love and rewards when there is no crying, so as to avoid teaching a child that crying gets him what he wants.

6. In general, rewards bring better results than punishment. So reasonable appreciation for his help (picking up toys or carrying a small sack of groceries from the car) and deserved praise for good behavior during some particular activity reinforces that behavior.

7. I am wondering just what role your husband plays in this little boy's life. Hopefully he spends quite a bit of time and is in complete unity with your disciplinary techniques. His time with your boy should be not only in play, but also in work, like having him help wash the car (with a sponge and a bucket of water to do the wheels) or taking part in his routine, like giving him his bath, reading to him, or putting him to bed. Also it would be well to have him get into some kind of special activity with his son like taking him out to see the stars just before he is tucked into bed. Hugs and kisses by both of you will come to be prized.

8. Children are born totally self-centered and the sooner you can help your child direct his interests outside himself, the better. If you can find a handicapped or old person to whom your little one could take a flower, some cookies, or a picture he makes and do it regularly, like once a week, it will help him learn the joy of helping others. I do not believe he is too young for this.

9. Whenever you know of a particular event ahead of time—company coming, a visit to the doctor, store or other errand—tell David exactly what you expect. If necessary, act out ahead of time what you and he will do. Then also let him know what the consequences will be if things do not go well. Our son told us later that he knew very well that it was "double jeopardy" if he should misbehave when we had company or when we were away from home. Our children were never fearful or insecure, but they knew their limits very well.

It is in the nature of children to try or test you as far as they can, and when their limits are not clearly defined, they are not secure. When they find they may not continually challenge your authority, they are more secure, happy children.

10. It is a law of children's minds that when you so firmly deny them a desired object as to remove all hope, their minds will soon cease to long for it and will be occupied in other pursuits. But as long as there is any hope of gaining the desired object, they will continue to try to obtain it.

11. And last but not least, prayer changes things, including both you and your child. Implore Jesus, who loves little children and has a special care for mothers, to help you cope with your little strong-willed boy. If you can "bend" his will properly, he can be a great power for good. I am sure God will give you the courage and the grace to do this.

Please let me know in three months or less how things are going. You cannot usually expect changes to happen overnight when it has taken months to develop the problems. Yet I hope that you will even see some changes in two or three days.

Blessings,

Dorothy Moore

P.S. Have you read Dr. Dobson's *The Strong-Willed Child*? Thomas Nelson will be publishing our new *Homebuilt Discipline* early next year, but in the meantime, you might also like to read Dr. Dobson's *Dare to Discipline*.

Bear in mind that this letter also involved telephone calls, and that Dorothy here laid down methods which would not only involve an eighteen-month-old boy, but would also apply as he grows in the months and years ahead. As you continue through this book you will be reminded by us and by your own convictions that you as well as your children have a lot to learn and that your self-control paves the way toward a smoother road in the control of your children.

Their First Five Years

We remind you that if you had a six-month-old colt you wouldn't saddle it and take it out on the race track. Nor would you take a three-week-old puppy to obedience school.

When human infants are born they are among the most helpless of all creatures. They have no judgment, no reasoning ability, and thus no knowledge on which to make choices. Since self-discipline is based on these abilities, you must provide the wisdom and judgment to make those choices. By judicious training, your children will become (1) mature in judgment, (2) able to reason consistently from cause to effect, and eventually (3) responsible for their own acts. This is your goal.

Soon after infants are born, they begin to learn. First, they find they are suddenly in a noisy, cold world, compared to the warm, cozy place they left when they squeezed out of the birth canal. Then they find Mommy's breasts and warmth and nourishment and hear her soft voice, to which they soon become conditioned and will recognize for the rest of their lives. Gradually they learn through their senses—taste, sight, hearing, smell, and touch: light and dark, loud and quiet, hard and soft, sour and sweet, bad and good, heat and cold, wet and dry, full and empty, comfort and pain. On each of these "learning hooks" they hang other learning, and soon they have a widening base for training and education, one which grows even broader, deeper, and faster as they learn to reason.

At birth, children have no experience and no basis for reasoning. They are little bundles of fatty tissue unlike you, who hopefully are packages of muscle. They are less able to take care of themselves in their sphere at six months or six years than a little chicken is six minutes out of the egg. Your newborn learns fast, but must develop "learning hooks," experiences on which to hang future learning. Although they learn very rapidly, their abilities to learn academic and social skills during their first three or four years is not nearly so great or quick and free as at eight or ten or twelve when they have developed thousands of learning hooks and some ability to reason with consistency.

What you do from day one has future consequences. Yet many parents wait until speech develops, not realizing that newborns understand parental management of their care as clearly as they ever will and know to what extent they will be indulged.

Given time, babies' instincts combine with intellectual growth so that before their first birthdays they will have you well "psyched out." Unless you take charge systematically, they will take charge of you—through crying, eating, bodily demands, and a thousand other instinctive inventions. Remember, they are not reasonable in their early years, so they will need loving firmness as you mold them into treasures of great value and build in values that stabilize them through their adolescent years.

Your tender consistency in actions and tone of voice provide the almost unconscious control needed in their early months. Yet remember, as we sketch through their developmental years, that children, *unlike animals,* vary as much as three or four years or more in developmental timing. Some seven-year-olds perform like five-year-olds or younger, others like nine-year-olds or older. Some children are reading at three or four, while others, *just as bright,* may not read until nine or ten or even later. In this book we deal with *average* developmental ages. But if there is any doubt about their maturity, it is better to wait than to rush.

Their First Year

Before your baby is born, you should decide who will be in control—you or your child. Watching other parents who answer their baby's every whim both day and night may help you in your determination. The thrill of a new baby can soon be dimmed by the fatigue that will undoubtedly overwhelm you by the demands of a yet untrained infant unless you are self-disciplined enough to be in control.

Since the newborn has no language skills by which you can lay down the ground rules for behavior, you will have to establish your training by your loving, but firm, consistent control of a reasonable routine of eating, sleeping, bathing, exercising, playing, and even loving—his rules in action, if you please. This commonsense schedule should be determined by your knowledge of the time needed for the digestive process between meals—usually three to four hours, the baby's weight at birth, his weight gain, and his natural body rhythms, as well as the needs of the rest of the family.

Remember that children are born without any habits. What you do with them in the first few weeks and months of their lives will establish sleeping and eating habits and attitudes that may be lifelong. Only a few repeated acts form habits, which operate automatically. Your gentle, imposed control before the baby is able to do so helps to develop *his* self-control. If you do not believe this and choose instead to allow your infant to be in control, you will help to perpetuate the pervasive qualities of this generation, described as self-centered, undisciplined, and demanding of immediate gratification—qualities that are natural at the newborn stage but unnatural for mature young people.

Mothers who distinguish and care for only the *real* needs of the newborn in contrast to his notions usually welcome the opportunity to face their daytime duties in a reasonably rested state. Since Baby does not know day from night, he doesn't mind playing, being walked, rocked, or fed while others are sleeping.

Hunger, indeed, is a real need, but appetite is trainable and is your responsibility. If he is offered food whenever he cries and often as a pacifier, he is likely to keep you more involved than you really want to be. Besides, he can easily come to believe that food is a cure for all ills and possibly develop an emotionally-based eating problem, which is widespread among adults in our society.

If your baby is six pounds or more, he can easily be trained to omit one middle-of-the-night feeding from day one with only minimal crying or fussing for a period of three nights or less, which will not cause emotional damage. This method also trains for good sleep patterns. A time of wakefulness and attention by the family in the afternoon or evening encourages a sound night's sleep.

A method which is used to manage night feedings without undue fatigue for the parents is the family bed, where baby sleeps with the parents until he is ready to leave. We have no research as to the effects of such a program, but it obviously would not fit everyone's lifestyle. Also the need for the extra feeding, or feedings, is questionable, for it keeps the digestive system working when it should have an extended time of rest, just as the body needs the longer night's sleep.

An ideal routine for a newborn should run something like the following and is the program on which our children were nurtured. They grew up to be healthy, emotionally secure, and obedient children. And Dorothy was a rested, unhassled Mommy who thoroughly enjoyed our children. Everyone we know who has consistently followed this plan has glowingly reported quiet, sweet-tempered babies developing into happy, obedient children with more equanimity and pleasure for their parents as well as a more organized home life. An added advantage is that if it becomes necessary for someone else to care for your baby, there is a plan to be followed. If for some good reason a three-hour feeding interval is necessary at birth, this is the approximate schedule you should work toward, at least by the age of three months:

6:00 A.M. Feeding—hopefully nursing on both breasts, assuming, of course, that Baby has wakened. Always give a full feeding, keeping baby awake by whatever means necessary, even diapering. If he awakens earlier, he can be fed but should wait until the regular time for the next feeding at 10:00 A.M.

6:30 A.M. or so. Change Baby's diaper and put him back to bed on his tummy for a nap. Advantages of "tummy" sleeping are (1) that it more nearly simulates his cuddly, natural position in the womb, (2) there is less chance of choking, (3) he can expel bubbles more easily, (4) studies demonstrate that it produces a better quality of sleep, and (5) it provides a disciplinary signal that says "now you are to go to sleep."

9:00 A.M. Waken Baby and undress him for exercise in warm room (ten to fifteen minutes) with loving attention and responses from Mother, as prelude to his bath.

10:00 A.M. Nursing.

10:30 A.M. Long nap, again on his tummy.

2:00 P.M. Nursing.

2:30 P.M. Time with family in infant seat, on clean blanket on floor, baby swing, or whatever. Baby may drop off for an hour or so but should not be allowed to sleep too long.

4:00 P.M. This seems to be the fussy time of day, and something different needs to be done to distract Baby—perhaps a time out of doors, a walk or a ride in the car on an errand with Mommy.

5:30 P.M. Exercise, perhaps a loving back rub before preparation for bed.

6:00 P.M. Nursing.

6:30 P.M. Bedtime—routine should consist of cuddling, songs, rhythmic reading (such as simple poems or rhymes with a lilt and repetition), rocking. It is preferable to put Baby in his bed while he is awake for the purpose of training so that he becomes accustomed to the routine as a matter of course and learns to accept it. He will resist, if you allow it, but after you check to be sure nothing legitimate is bothering him, he should be left without any further attention—that is, unless you are willing to rock, walk, or submit to his ideas for several years to come.

10:00 P.M. Nursing.

Adaptations to the above suggestions may be made to fit the family's needs, as long as they are consistent. Whatever the plan, it should preferably be put down on paper and then altered as the baby grows. If it seems best that Daddy and the older children see and respond to Baby during family breakfast making and breakfast, he could nap instead of having a bath at 9:00 A.M. and his bath could be at 5:00 or 5:30 P.M. at his restless time.

Also his time with Daddy and the family could be between 6:30 and 8:00 P.M. instead of in the afternoon, especially if the whole family chooses to get to bed early. In this case his nap would come at 2:30 P.M. And if Mother also prefers an early bedtime, which could be of inestimable value to her, Baby's 10:00 P.M. feeding could be postponed until he wakens at 11:00 or 12:00, which of course may lengthen his sleeptime through the night.

You will notice that if there is to be flexibility in the feeding routine, it is most appropriate with the last feeding at night and the first feeding in the morning, for indeed the little one cannot read the clock. Yet you will find that his rhythm will soon be so firmly established that he is almost as accurate as an alarm clock!

From ten to fourteen days old up to three months, a normal baby will gain an average of about an ounce a day and weigh somewhere from eleven to thirteen pounds. After that, weight gain will slow to about five ounces a week until he is about six months old, during which time he will likely double his birth weight. If he has not already done so, he can be eased into only four feedings a day, particularly with the introduction of some solid foods. And by the age of one year he can be on three meals a day.

Remember that Baby has many needs besides food and these needs should be lovingly fulfilled. If your baby seems hungry before time for his feeding, distract him the best you can with singing, swinging, or even walking, which is far better in the daytime than at night. Water in a bottle should be offered at wake times *between meals* even if your baby is breastfed, for he needs to learn to like water and, especially in warm weather, he probably needs it. If you start this while Baby is very young, even soon after birth, he is likely to accept the artificial nipple more readily. In case there should ever be an emergency, it is well to have Baby willing to take a bottle.

Such regularity and firmness along with your loving daytime cuddling and attention are important basic steps in discipline and help your youngster become an organized person. All babies in good health are well prepared to adapt to a regular program, though some will be easier than others. Except in cases of illness or other neonatal adjustment problems, gentle persistence will produce a disciplined, happy child.

But if you do not tenderly maneuver your infant to reasonably conform to your well-considered program, he will train you to fit into his whims and unreasoning notions. To bow to a baby's whims and even discomfort by providing food in a permissive manner will produce a demanding, self-willed (often construed to be strong-willed) child, to say nothing of the damage the food itself may bring to the child's health from adding new food to the digestive system which has not yet finished its last job with rest in between—a common, but not the only, cause of colic. It is now known that cow's milk used by the mother during pregnancy and while nursing can also cause colic.

Although a few disagree, some strongly, all of those who write Dorothy after trying these principles and methods are in striking agreement and have exciting results. We wish we could include several of these letters here, but we will give you at least one from a Florida mother and one from a Massachusetts father.

A MOTHER'S TESTIMONY ON TRAINING BABIES TO SLEEP ALL NIGHT

When I delivered my second baby, I was still waking up to the cries of my eleven-month-old, one and two times a night. I told my doctor that "I guess there is no point in going to bed at night, with two baby girls to get up at night with." He expressed surprise. He told me that he and his wife had nine healthy, beautiful children and he wouldn't let her get up at night to feed them. I said, "Don't they need to eat at night to grow, and don't they get hungry?" He said, "If you want to gain weight, do you have to get up at night to do it?" I assured him that I didn't. I get all the calories I need in the day. He told me a baby may eat a little more in the day or in a growth spurt, perhaps more often, but that a baby needs the sleep at night as much as the food in order to be a happy, well-adjusted, healthy baby.

I was taught by my 39-year-old doctor, with nine beautiful children, to give my baby a final feeding about 10:00 P.M. Then, every time she woke up until about 5:00 A.M., he encouraged me to offer the baby purified water. He said they train the baby to wake up at night in the hospital when they give them milk, but it is just a habit, not a necessity. In desperation for my own health after two babies in two years and little sleep, I put it to a test and boy, did it work like a charm! He told me it might take two or three nights to retrain the baby and it did. I also started giving my eleven-month-old, Jennifer, water in her bottle. Was she mad at me! Even threw the bottle at the wall, she was so

73

insulted to have water after 11 months of cream. After a week or two of water (she was well-trained for milk), Jennifer was sleeping all night and so was our newborn, Michelle, on her third night at home. "Mommy" became a new person too, and did I ever feel rested and enjoy being a mother! Even had enough energy to rock and play with my babies.

The results have been wonderful. Babies with great temperaments turn into beautiful young women with great temperaments. When they are sick, they sleep well at night. Doctors will tell you that your body heals twice as fast when it is resting. We have six precious daughters and are so grateful for the principle of rest taught in the Bible of "early to bed, early to rise," and when we get enough rest, we truly can be ambassadors for our Savior and use our energy in service before Him.

—FLORIDA

DON'T CRY, SWEETHEART. DADDY LOVES YOU

When our first child was born, we were not really sure what to do. However, the reasons that were shared for letting a child "set his own schedule" seemed like the thing to do. So, we decided to let our son be the one who decided when he should eat. My wife was breast feeding the baby, and what followed were two weeks of very unpleasant experiences with our child's feeding schedule. He chose to eat about every hour and a half to two hours, and it was very physically and emotionally draining on my wife.

At the end of two weeks, we were scheduled to meet with our pediatrician for our first visit. Prior to our decision to select him as our pediatrician, I had phoned him and talked with him for the specific purpose of learning about his background, experience, and general philosophical approach to raising children. He had been highly recommended, and, after our conversation, I was very much impressed with him as someone who was knowledgeable of his field and had a good deal of practical experience. (He and his wife were the parents of six children.) To our surprise, he strongly encouraged us to put our son on a firm feeding schedule.

He mentioned that as long as a child was over 6 lbs. (with no other complicating factors), he was physically capable of going $3\frac{1}{2}$ to 4 hours between feedings, with one extended period in each 24-hour cycle. He felt that it was definitely better for the baby to go that long between feedings in order to provide time for the child's body to digest the milk already taken before eating again. He also felt it was better for the mother, because it would enable her to plan time to do other things, especially when there is more than one child in the home. I wondered how long it would take to establish a four-hour schedule for our son, and he assured us that children are able to adapt very quickly to the world around them. He was quite sure that it would only take from 3 days to a week.

After thinking through the issue more carefully than we had before, and with the added assurance from our pediatrician that feeding on a schedule was medically sound, we decided to follow his advice. We kept a record of when our child cried, and for how long, and phoned our pediatrician each morning to make sure that what was happening was all right. He assured us, each time, that everything was fine. After 3 days, our son was adapting quite well to the schedule, and, after a week, he just didn't cry anymore for food. He was a very happy baby who earned the nickname "Wonderful William" from a number of our friends because he was such a contrast to a number of other children who cried quite often—their way of "demanding" food, as well as other things.

With our second and third children, we began the scheduling at the hospital right after they were born. My wife experienced a considerable amount of pressure from the nursing staff of the hospital to feed our second child on demand, but, with the positive experience we had with our first child and with the continued assurance of our pediatrician, she withstood the pressure. In each case, there was very little crying at all when we arrived home from the hospital. Our third child is now about 3½ months old, and a friend recently commented to me, after observing her contentedly sitting in her infant carrier, "Boy, George, you just seem to get happy babies!" I'm beginning to wonder how many children we'll have to have before people realize that it doesn't just "happen."

The question which we think is at the heart of the issue is who really knows better what is best for the child—the child or the parents? We had initially assumed that the child knew his needs best; thus, he should be the one to determine the feeding schedule. However, after some more mature reflection on the subject, and after observing how our son made his decisions, it was quite obvious that his decisions were based on "felt" needs, not real needs, and he was motivated by purely selfish reasons. As parents, after consulting with our pediatrician, we knew much better than he did what his real needs for nourishment were, and we also were concerned with the "best interests" not only of him, but of others as well.

We have also become convinced that, as responsible parents, we need to look ahead to the future in order to lay the foundations, in principle, for behavior which will be required of our children later. For, in a very real sense, it is cruel to allow our children to develop habits unnecessarily which we know will have to be broken later. At some time in their lives, children must learn to eat at specific times, along with others. They must also learn that they don't get things by screaming and "demanding." In the area of personal character development, it is important for children to learn that they don't always get what they want, when they want it, regardless of the impact of their desire on others. It is also important to instill in them a sense of trust in and respect for their parents, so that their security is based on something far more solid than their own ability to direct the affairs of life.

One very important lesson relating to my own personal life was impressed on me while we were first teaching our son the schedule we had planned for him. He was crying, and, as I comforted him while we waited for the upcoming feeding time, I kept saying, "Don't cry, Sweetheart. Daddy loves you. He would never let you be hurt by not feeding you at the right time." As I encouraged my little boy with those words, I was reminded that the same principle applies with regard to my walk with God. Although His provision is sure, because He is wiser than I, His timetable sometimes differs from mine.

Over the past few years, my wife and I have become increasingly convinced that scheduled feeding is clearly superior to feeding "on demand." It is better for the baby's health. It is better for the baby's social and character development. And it is better for the parents and the rest of the family. There is far less crying, and far more peace and joy for everyone in the house.

—MASSACHUSETTS

During their first year your children will grow in many ways. They will learn to turn over, to grab, to sit, to crawl, to pull themselves up, to walk with your help, to handle and manipulate things that you show them: reaching, grasping, putting things in their mouths. As they learn to walk—sometimes before the first year's end and often months later—they will often fall, but they are well cushioned with flesh and fat, instead of muscle like you, so don't worry.

Their sleep time at first will occupy most of the day. Even by the end of their first year, they are still sleeping twelve to fourteen hours out of twenty-four, including one or two daytime naps at regular times. Since babies differ in sleep needs, your judgment is adequate to decide on their real needs, especially if you have already trained them to good sleep habits.

Your babies will communicate by looking at you, responding

by fear or affection, depending on your tone and their comfort. They learn gestures as you wave "Hi" or "Bye-bye," and responses to words, such as the meaning of "No." They speak by crying, gurgling, and babbling sounds, using tones to express their feelings, until they learn words and more sophisticated communication *by imitating you*.

You will see their reasoning develop as they follow movements with their eyes, recognize people, and respond to your smiles or scowls. They will learn to hold a cracker, eat it, and eventually hold a cup without your help and drink with little help. They will hold out their arms to you and stretch their legs while you are dressing them.

Socially, your children will learn to initiate their smiles as they differentiate between friends and strangers and to recognize their own names. They will clearly react to "Yes" and "No," especially "No." And they will mimic you and others freely.

Once again, remember that little children, like animals, are more trained than educated. They have yet to learn to reason, and they do not have the powerful instincts of a bright dog; they need even more patience and understanding than an animal. As they grow older they will need less repetition and more reason. But for now, repetition and routine are among their best sources of security and are necessary aids to their mental and emotional development.

Their Second Year

At the outset of their second year, your children's most obvious occupation may be learning how to walk, first with you, then alone, then even backwards. They will learn to pick up things without falling, will keep time to music, pull and push toys, and play with coordination toys—putting rings on poles, large pegs in pegboards, and blocks on top of one another.

Some two-year-olds become quite skilled at turning pages and scribbling, especially with large crayons or chalk, although it will be several years before they can handle pencil and lined paper with any skill. They coordinate hands and arms as they finger-paint or toss a ball or turn doorknobs. But they may tire easily, and in any event should have regular daily naps, for some both morning and afternoon, depending on family bedtime, which we hope will be early.

At this point, you may need to guide their curiosity and their desire to explore. To minimize your "no's," it is wise to child-proof your house by removing dangerous items and also valuable or breakable objects. Then patience, repetition, and consistency must reign as you help your child learn his limits — *just because you say so* — for he simply can't understand "why" even if you explained over and over again. Though he can be trained to be very obedient (just as a dog can be trained not to cross a boundary in a house), he is *not* self-controlled and must be under your watchful eye to keep him and your household safe and under control.

At eighteen months, our grandchild, Bryon, was very curious about the dishwasher and made himself a nuisance whenever his mother unloaded it. So she decided to change her technique from getting him out of the way to involving him. She allowed him to hand her one dish at a time to put away, a routine which took more than twice her time. Next she decided to put her plastic dishes, which were virtually unbreakable, in a low cupboard and her tableware in a drawer so Bryon could reach them. Now he could do it all. In the process he learned to sort, stack and eventually load the dishwasher. Who could say who was prouder of his accomplishment, Bryon or his mother?

Two-year-olds learn to understand such words and phrases as *where? on, in, under, on top, over there,* and can carry out simple orders such as "[Please] get Daddy's slippers" or "Give me the pencil," or even a simple series of instructions such as "Please pick up your spoon and give it to Mother."

They are now beginning to talk, to say their first meaningful words, although for some, speech may be delayed until their second year or later, even for normal and bright children. They become possessive and use *my* or *mine,* and can say a lot in a word or two such as *more* or *all gone*. By age two, your children may be able to speak clearly twenty-five to one hundred words. Their reason is beginning to blossom noticeably so that they can ask questions.

As we said before, children are great imitators. If they mimic you when you get after them or give them instructions, they are not necessarily being sassy, at least at first. They are learning to express themselves and will do as you do in content and tone. They like to hear their names and should learn their importance as time goes on. Important steps include giving simple, acceptable choices of which dish to eat from, which book to read, without allowing them to rule you or too many areas of their lives. Such choices set the stage for later decision making.

Two-year-olds have developed some physical balance and like to be in and near the action—your cooking, sewing, laundry, dishwashing, bed making—but their attention span is sharply limited. They like to explore for themselves, need to work out their own imaginations—in sand piles, by the stream or lake, in the kitchen with you—which will become even more imaginative in the next few years.

Your children are now coordinated enough to take off their shoes and clothes and begin to learn how to wash and dry their hands and faces. Youngsters this age watch others in curiosity but are not social creatures, preferring side-by-side parallel play.

Now is the time to begin teaching them order. If you do this consistently, you will save yourself endless picking up after them. Rather, let them learn to pick up after *you* to a reasonable degree—pick up the fly swatter, put your shoes in their rack and the broom in the closet. They will learn to put their things away—blocks, books, toys, clothes—if you work consistently to help them develop this habit—which can avoid no end of problems and strain on you.

Avoid asking, "Would you like to . . . ?" or "Do you want to . . . ?" unless you have a way to get around a negative answer, which is typical of the two-year-old's desire for independence. Though a necessary step in development, such autonomy can get out of hand if you are not clever enough to work around it and even use it to your advantage by managing to do *his* things with him as much as possible.

Their Third Year

By age three children are becoming highly physical, with good balance and coordination; they can throw and kick balls, run, jump, and walk tiptoe. This accelerated activity necessitates an hour or two daily naptime despite their increase in age. You will find this an important economy that assists in their discipline, whether or not the neighbor's kids are doing it. It will help you to take a nap with them.

Their fine muscle coordination is improving, so they can string large beads, use scissors to cut paper (but without accuracy) and hold crayons or chalk with their thumbs and forefingers instead of their fists. Three-year-olds continue to learn by touching, tasting, and feeling rather than by asking questions. However, they do add the word *what. Why, how,* and *how much* will come later for most children.

Some children are getting elimination under control, especially girls, although other children may have to be diapered at night for another year or two, particularly boys, who mature generally at a slower rate than girls.

As your youngsters' reasoning powers unfold, you will want to help them understand *why* they should obey. They can partially understand at least that little animals and birds obey their parents in order to be safe. You can illustrate this in real life or by stories. For example, baby chicks come quickly when their mother says, "Cluck, cluck," and a baby fawn learns to stay very still in order to be safe.

You should help them understand other safety reasons. Through cause and effect experiences, they may already understand such cautions as why they should not touch the stove. The danger of running into or across the street can also be taught by stories or demonstrated in real life when you see an animal which has been run over in the street. Make use of everyday happenings to help your child develop his understanding. There is reason to believe that privileged children—those who have a great deal of parental response—proceed faster through cognitive stages than "average" or deprived children.

Respect for privacy and ownership, first among family members and then others, is a valuable early learning and will help to avoid many problems. By gentle reminders and appreciation, teach your child to comply by always knocking before opening a closed door. And give each child a place or places of his own with tender instruction not to get into others' belongings. Very early your explanations should be "No, no, that is Daddy's" or "No, no, that is Kelly's." It is simple to ask them if they want you or big brother to take their things. Or to say that if you take Kelly's things, then he should be able to take yours.

They are beginning to enjoy more stories, both told and read, and may want to hear the same stories dozens of times. This repetitive process is an important informal exercise as a preparation for learning to read because it helps them to establish their mental channels, their "learning hooks." They put together many bits of information about cars, planes, household items, to attach to these learning hooks.

They will like trips out of the house, especially with Daddy before bedtime to look at the moon and the stars. Imaginations are becoming vivid. Although they are not yet truly sociable creatures in the sense of working and playing unselfishly together, they are becoming more conforming and anxious to please, more interested in you and in others, and more likely to listen when you suggest that they share. However, they are not likely to be tidy unless you have consistently trained them to be.

At mealtime one day, Dorothy's experience with our three-year-old grandson clearly demonstrates a young child's ability to carry out instructions. She put a nut-cheese spread on a slice of bread and cut it into four pieces so he could handle it well. When he picked up one piece to eat it, he put nearly the entire piece in his mouth. So she said, "Brent, you are taking too big bites. Please take the next piece in four bites." But though he was a cooperative little fellow, he did the same thing again. When she mildly remonstrated with him and asked why he didn't do "what Grandma said," he answered, "I don't know how to make four bites." And indeed, he didn't. This particular concept was still beyond him. He was not yet capable of following her instructions on numbers.

Three-year-olds talk a lot to get your attention and respect. They may show some temper as a demonstration of their courage or inability to get you to listen, possibly because of a new member in the family—baby or father or mother. These children are likely to show resentment to a new baby if you have not "planned" the new arrival *with* them well in advance and have not helped them to realize that baby brother or sister belongs to *them*.

Don't necessarily judge them as hostile if they throw a rock at someone. They are experimenting with coordination. Give them something safe to throw at and throw with them. Insist that they don't throw rocks at anybody at any time. Yet in that teaching process, remember that if you yell at them not to throw while they are in the act of throwing, they may not be able to stop, simply because their brain circuits are slow and immature.

Their Fourth Year

Your young ones are now developing coordination which amounts to a certain poise. They are hopping on one foot, walking on a line, riding a tricycle, jumping over a curb, and landing with both feet together. They can throw a ball overhand and even catch a large ball at short range. They are learning to use hammers, saws, kitchen tools; they can fill the dishwasher or wash dishes in the sink. Now they can become cooks, helping you to fill cups of flour to make cookies. They like to help Daddy wash the car, especially the wheels. This constructive work *with you* is their highest form of play, so encourage them even though the chore takes twice as long to complete. Because of their increased activity, they continue to need daily midday rest.

Hopefully four-year-olds are beginning to be sociable, sharing, demanding less attention to themselves. Yet they are restless, often aggressive, and sometimes, in a child's way, obscene. They quickly pick up naughty words, signs, and acts, possibly exposing genitals, playing "house" with members of the opposite sex, and even urinating indiscreetly outside. This does not mean they are abnormal in their sex interests, but more likely that they will try almost anything for recognition and to show independence.

At four, children play with either sex, but prefer their own. Now they become extremely imitative and vulnerable to peer approval and therefore to peer dependency, which is pervasive even at preschool levels. Play with agemates should be limited for these reasons, and tendencies to overexcitement will need to be watched. They may seem to enjoy their playmates when often they are just trying to please and thus are under additional strain. Their natural tendency to mimic now develops into the ability to dramatize stories, by pretending to be animals or Mommy or Daddy. "Make believe" is great fun, and children at this age like to begin a sentence with *what if.* . . .

At this age children of both sexes often may become cruel in actions and remarks, with boys more likely to be bullies. The more they are with you (assuming your responses are warm) and the less with groups of children, the less likely they are to become aggressive, unpleasant, and undisciplined. One way or another they will assert their own importance, a factor which you can handle best away from the competition of play-mates. You will find that they are more likely to respond nega-tively to your corrections if they have just spent a good deal of time with peers with whom they had to struggle for recogni-tion.

Four-year-olds are beginning to learn concepts of time: the meaning of "yesterday" and "tomorrow." They understand size comparisons: which is bigger and smaller, which is more or less. You can expect them to understand your explanations better, although they may not reason consistently until around the ages of eight to ten.

These children can distinguish and appreciate different col-ors. They are also drawing and coloring better, so that others besides you can recognize their pictures. Yet you should not expect much of their fine muscle coordination. Boys will be even slower than girls in developing these skills.

You can expect four-year-olds to know their own first and last names and ages, and sometimes their addresses. Phone numbers may have to wait a year or so. They can also learn a desirable independence by using the toilet, buttoning clothes, blowing their noses, washing their hands, buttering bread, and pouring water or milk unassisted. Many youngsters can even tie shoes at this age, particularly if taught by another child rather than by you.

Reasoning ability continues to blossom, but though your lit-tle ones' brilliant remarks may please and amaze you, don't be fooled into believing that they can be very consistent or understanding. Continuing to choose between two acceptable actions helps them develop ability to weigh acceptable alternatives in making decisions. For instance, allow them to decide whether you will go today (or tomorrow) to visit the park or the fire station. Or whether your child wants to wear his blue or his green shirt.

Principles of right and wrong, safety, and treatment of others, including sharing, must be taught by precept and example. They do not develop naturally. If you are proud that your four-year-old is kind or generous, it is more likely that he senses this in you than that he is naturally that way. We do recognize that children differ in personality and that training "takes" more easily with some, but in general their senses are so sharp that they "catch" much more than they are taught.

Stories of obedience and the consequences of disobedience read or told by you of incidents in your life or the lives of others help to cement your consistent example. Our grandchildren never tire of hearing Grandma Dorothy tell about their Mommy (Kathie) when she was a little girl of twenty months—how her Daddy (Grandpa Ray) hurried away from the ocean liner headed for Hawaii to buy her a little harness before we weighed anchor. She explains how this was to allow Kathie some freedom to run without danger of falling overboard when she was too young to know better and that rules, including God's rules, are like Kathie's harness—to keep us from making serious or harmful mistakes.

Another favorite story is about when we tied Kathie up because she went to the neighbor's more than once without asking. She was told that little puppies don't know any better so we have to tie them up. She had a blanket in the yard to play on with a few toys. Bryon and Brent especially like Grandma's surprise when Kathie made herself so happy in her "punishment" that the little neighbor boy who stopped by to see her went home and asked his mother to tie him up.

Guard carefully the senses which pick up the bad more easily than the good whether by television, peers, or other influences. Young children do not have the ability to sort out or choose the good from the bad.

In case you are tempted to resort to nursery or preschool because of pressure from relatives or friends, consider well the risks in terms of breaking down the parent-child bond or of picking up the bad manners, language or habits of other children as well as diseases and becoming peer dependent even at this early age, which is a more common problem than you might realize. Who will set the pace and teach your children's values? Their agemates? Or you? Would you send your pedigreed dog out with the pack? Remember that all the training of an obedience course can go down the drain in one fling with the pack.

Their Fifth Year

Your children are now inclined to become more independent of family ties. If you provide a consistent example, working and playing and serving others with them, their loyalties will grow closer to you. But if you delegate—or relegate—them to the care and companionship of others, you will weaken your ties with them and, of course, your control. They will be less likely to become self-controlled and well-disciplined and more likely to become disrespectful and abusive.

Still, no matter how careful and consistent you are, there will be times when your children may seem overly dependent. Their struggle for security does not come automatically. Of course, you will see dependency on you for those expedient things, which they cannot secure from others—food, clothes, and transportation—and it is possible they may even use you. But in general children who have time with you and therefore confidence in your loving interest, your imaginative questions, and your accurate responses feel secure enough to be reasonably independent. You can now *begin* to use the words *why, how,* and *when* as well as *what* and *where,* and expect them to understand: why they behave as they do (whether happy or angry), why spiders spin webs (for housing and to catch insects), how you hammer nails or follow a recipe. They can begin developing a sense of time, of day and night and of seasons.

If you surrender them to an institution or day-care group at this early age, they may cling to you as if fearful of losing you. Eventually you may even feel threatened as their loyalty to their playmates and devotion to their teachers or caretakers subtracts from their concern for you and your control of their behavior. This is almost certain to happen if their association is with an unselected group of children who do not abide by your values. If you unwisely defend your children's attitudes or punish the children without your spouse's approval when your spouse disapproves of them, your children will become a continual source of disagreement between you.

Five-year-olds are developing quite mature balance. For example, they can walk a balance beam with some ease. They like to climb ropes, ladders, rocks, trees. Their fine-muscle coordination is gradually growing so that they may want to cut paper and write letters. Girls especially may become skillful enough to cut paper continuously on a line, print letters clearly, and copy across a page during the next year or two. But boys more often may be slower and less interested.

They still continue to need a daily nap, we believe, to avoid the temper tantrums that result from being overly tired. At this age, children like to make comparisons: big, bigger, biggest; or pretty and prettiest. You can expect them to understand a sequence of instructions, which means that they can have some specific duties like planning to go to the stores, but making sure that all things are put away first.

They enjoy stories as much or more than ever, and to retell them, yet because of their combination of inexperience and imagination, they may often misinterpret the facts. It is both fun and profitable for you to discuss the story or experience and bring it into perspective and in line with truth. They will be more than a little silly sometimes when talking, listening, or playing, especially when two or three of them are together. Smile, but talk commonsense to them; don't get silly with them or encourage silliness.

Continue to teach the basic reasons why we do what we do, which form the principles of behavior. On the basis of this information, their knowledge of these principles of health, work, neatness, treatment of others, language, and manners, you can help your child to make more and more decisions affecting himself and the family, allowing him to use his own self-control wherever you can depend on him to make desirable decisions. Extend this privilege gradually through the coming years as reasonability increases, but bear in mind that consistency in reasoning is not fully mature until ages ten to twelve and that development of total self-discipline is a lifelong process.

◥◥◥◥◥◥◥◥◥◥◥◥◥◥ 7 ◤◤◤◤◤◤◤◤◤◤◤◤◤◤
Their Transition Years: Six to Eight

Although we in no way deride teenage development, the six to eight ages are in some ways your years-of-last-resort in the development of controls and values in your young. Once they are past age eight and into the prepubescent years of nine to twelve, so many things are happening in their race to adulthood that you will not be able to hang on unless you have conditioned yourself—and them—years before. It is hardly a time to be sending them off to an institution unless absolutely necessary. In all events we should spend every minute we possibly can with them as their very personal friends.

Children vary widely in their maturity during these years—as much as three or four years. Girls will generally be a year or so ahead of boys developmentally. These transition years are usually a period of rapid physical development in preparation for accelerated mental growth. Yet do not make the mistake of feeling that early childhood is over. Because school is traditionally provided for all at age six simply for economic and political reasons, society has been tempted to consider "school age" as the beginning of middle childhood. On the contrary, sixes and sevens and sometimes eights have much the same qualities as children under six and share the same developmental tasks.[1]

Children at this age can run lightly on their toes, jump broadly, skip rope, ride two-wheeler bikes, roller-skate, and handle a ball with facility. Their fine-muscle coordination is now growing rapidly, so you can expect them to handle a pencil like an adult and learn to trace and cut accurately. By this age they will begin to use one hand more than the other. If they show a tendency toward left-handedness, don't worry. Be patient, and, in this case, let nature take its course.

Your youngsters are now coming out of infancy and should be expected to talk more clearly, use good grammar, and take appropriate turns in conversation, although good manners dictate that children give conversational priorities to adults. Their language, as one writer said it, should be pure and kind and true, the outward evidence of an inward grace. That likelihood will depend largely upon your speech and actions. If you have a problem with your grammar, get a game that you can play with your children.[2]

These are *pre*academic years, a period when they should be getting their physical and emotional act together before formal schooling, sometime after age eight. There is no replicated research in the United States or elsewhere that suggests that normal children are ready for formal schooling before ages eight to twelve.[3] Such top learning authorities as Tufts University's David Elkind and University of California's (Berkeley) William Rohwer observe that we could save millions of learning failures and child burnouts if we would delay formal schooling until the junior high school years.

Psychologists generally consider six- to eight-year-olds to have three basic needs: achievement, autonomy, and recognition by their peers. Yet this depends largely upon parental values and the meaning they assign to those basic needs. Achievement in what? How much autonomy? What kind of peer recognition and approval?

Character development should be your highest goal through their earlier years and must now become their highest achievement. This is not a putdown on academic skills — which have their important place but which should not be placed above the development of your children's basic value system.

Autonomy is good and important as long as it leads to the kind of self-direction that is born of genuine *self-worth*. We do not speak here of the typical *self-esteem* syndrome of the day, which emphasizes ego more than the selflessness of genuine self-respect. Nor do we stress child independence of parents nor that child license which grants freedom without responsibility.

Peer approval of the highest quality is gained only through the development of self-respect and self-direction, which operates independently of the peer culture. This is best developed at home where children learn to feel needed, wanted, and depended upon as they share family responsibilities and learn key skills in constructive study, work, and service *with you*.

At this age children should be lengthening their attention spans and powers of concentration. They are refining and developing consistency in their ability to reason, but they are not yet cognitively mature—genuinely able to reason consistently from cause to effect. You should bear this clearly in mind when school lessons are recommended that require consistent formal thought processes. This is one of the most certain ways to frustrate and burn out children of this age, especially boys.

Their young brains are beginning to *lateralize;* that is, the two hemispheres of the brain are getting closer to the years in which they will almost perfectly complement each other. One hemisphere or side of the brain is more analytical; the other side is more verbal and creative. If allowed to develop naturally, there will be a balance which most children today do not enjoy. Furthermore, until at least age ten or twelve, if a child receives brain damage in one hemisphere, there is a much greater chance that the other hemisphere will compensate to a remarkable degree. This is unlikely to happen after age twelve.

Until at least age eight and for many children, ten to twelve, their senses—taste, touch, smell, vision, hearing—do not mature enough for formal learning assignments that continue for several hours a day as in conventional schools. This is possibly the single biggest cause for learning disability today, yet the school systems of the Western world, aided by teacher associations, publishers, and ignorant or indifferent parents, pursue the idea of early schooling as if it were going to bring genius. In fact, the *Smithsonian* reported that it does just the opposite.[4]

The normal inclination at this age is for the child to begin replacing parents with peers as his or her companions and arbiters of values. Often clubs or gangs are the principal modes. In any event peer pressures from spending more time with agemates than parents create alienation from parents, loss of respect for adults, especially parents, loss of self-worth, and even loss of trust in their own peers.

Whenever possible you should be sharing more of your children's active daily hours than should their peers, at least until they are about age twelve. Otherwise children will not be self-directed as you hope or adopt your values. Their peers will reign. It is no coincidence that *Bar Mitzvah*—at age thirteen—was considered the age of responsibility in ancient times.

Today the cruel scourge of peer dependency is felt in every generation from preschool through adulthood, robbing society of truly creative, independent, morally strong citizens and laying before us pathetic people who, not thinking for themselves, must eat, dress, entertain, and otherwise do as they perceive others doing. Strengthening and perpetuating this peer culture is the grit and muscle and livelihood of the modern advertising industry.

Your consistent fellowship and example is the best antidote for peer dependency. Children of this age like to feel independent and important in the family and in their dealings with their peers. Yet you do not want them to become unnecessarily independent of you nor self-important. The best way to build the right kind of independence and importance is to have them with you more than with their peers, active in work and service, feeling that you need and depend upon them. Be sure to allow them to help make their rules at this age; they are more likely to abide by such rules.

Sex Roles

Another developmental pattern strongly affected by modern trends is the role difference between boys and girls and the efforts of feminists, gays, and others to develop a unisex culture. Normally girls tend to be much less physically aggressive than boys and spend more of their time with girls. In many circles—churches, schools, clubs, sporting events—there are strong efforts to close this gap. We believe such efforts to make boys more like girls and girls more like boys are dangerous, with both of them often uncertain of their roles, which is likely to bring uncertainty, unhappiness, worry, and sometimes arrogance and impulsiveness. This does not mean that boys should not help in the kitchen or that girls should not assist in the garage or garden. It means in simple old-fashioned terms to let girls be girls and boys be boys.

Your seven- or eight-year-old may become quite an actor, and all his world is his stage. Some of his acting may be a bit bizarre. He may not know the difference between silliness or naughty talk and ordinary humor, or between cruelty and fun. Be patient: his judgment is growing, but is not yet mature. Your close attention to his needs—more than his wants—and your consistent, warm response, encouragement, and example will help him to know the difference between wisdom and foolishness.

Other Associates

You need to have a great deal of the authority in determining the kinds of friends with whom your children associate, for their friendships have far-reaching effects. When decisions are to be made regarding activities even as simple as playing with

94

a neighborhood child, discuss ahead of time the relationship, in terms of its influence on your child, his leadership or lack of leadership in providing a good example in his play, obligations or chores to which your child may need to give priority before or after play, and time limitations. This helps him set his standard of behavior and establish his criteria for association with others. And it will be easier for him—and you—if he is a rested child, preferably with an early bedtime or a daily nap.

When our children were in their transition years, they enjoyed playing with a family very dear to us. But soon we saw some changes in their behavior that scared us—a new kind of selfishness we had not seen before. Then we began to realize what was happening. Our friends were very wealthy; they gave their children anything they wanted when they wanted it. We, of course, could not keep up, nor did we intend to. This became one factor in our moving to another part of the state.

In these childhood associations, your children will reflect almost precisely the behavior of those children or adults who are with them most. Sometimes it will be costly to set your lifestyle in the right direction, but doing so will cost you much less in the long run. We knew that if our children did not turn from snobbery and selfishness at that crucial age, the battle would be much harder later. We had to choose between closest friends—and sometimes relatives—with their Cokes, TV, snacking, and shows and God's beckoning to a wholesome future. For some of our friends this has meant fewer trips even to Grandpa and Grandma and Uncle and Aunt. If that must be, it must be, for Mother and Dad are accountable, no one else.

8

From Childhood to Adolescence: Nine to Teenage

Between their ninth and twelfth years, your children are awakening to a new world, including maturing of the senses, improved coordination, consistent reasonability, balanced brain function, and hormonal changes with the beginnings of potential sex functions—usually earlier in girls than in boys.

Now there is less confusion about sex roles. In boys there is much more inclination to be dominant, skillful, strong—even daring, and there is a hint of developing femininity in girls. Yet the permissiveness of the last twenty or thirty years, the emphasis on sex for sex's sake, explicit sex in the media, sex "education" in classrooms and in social circles and even in churches, has created a sexual awareness, which has brought earlier sexual maturity in both sexes. As a result, secondary sex characteristics—breasts, pubic and armpit hair—may show up earlier in this period. Your children need a frank understanding of these changes and their implications for their future happiness, and they need them from you! Your authority is already in jeopardy at this age and will most certainly suffer if you leave such information to their peers or other adults.

It may surprise you that these years of nine to twelve or thirteen are at first a plateau or a rest period in physical development before your children begin, usually later in this period, a time of rapid growth, first in height and then in weight. The girls' rate of maturity is even greater now, often as much as two years ahead of boys. Also during this period girls are often taller than boys of the same age.

96

There is much teasing within and between sexes. Yet there is warm and appropriate affection and a sense of humor if you have set the example. Don't be surprised if they seem awkward, restless, even lazy, which can be caused by their rapid and uneven growth. They may worry you with critical, changeable, uncooperative, or even rebellious times, although these will be minimized if you are involving them intimately in household planning, including the management of money. Preteens are interested in pets, games, technological advances, and—if you are not careful—will give undue attention to radio, television, and the comics. They need you more than any of these.

Most of their baby fat is now gone. Some of the uneven and rapid growth will be seen in the body contours as boys become broader in their shoulders and the girls more shapely in their hips. With this growth often come enormous though capricious appetites. The girls, because of their earlier maturity, often seem more interested in boys than boys are in them.

Don't be surprised if your preteens are defensive about their friends or otherwise assert their independence. They are reaching out—to gangs, clubs, church groups. If it ever becomes a question of need either for your camaraderie or of the association of their agemates, never forget that *peer* association can usually be sacrificed without damage to them, but they must not get along without *you*. If you follow our suggestions for warmth, consistency, work, and service when your children are younger, they will respect you.

Build their self-worth not only in these ways, but also through careful education in manners, cleanliness, and order, particularly during this time when there may be an inclination toward carelessness or slovenliness. They now can reason consistently and will understand you if you lovingly and firmly give them a share in making the rules of your home. Remember that they are able to pick up after you at least as much as you once picked up after them, particularly as they grow older and accumulate more responsibilities. Now is the time for you to prepare them to be the kind of parents you want them to be.

The Golden Rule is an excellent measure and guide at this point. Try to avoid unkind or unnecessary intrusion into their affairs, but by appreciation, encouragement, and loving, but firm, guidance, unobtrusively let them sense that you are still their very special parents and that their security still lies largely with you. Do things with them—picnics, camping, family outings—and occasionally invite other families whose standards are not in conflict with yours. You are setting the stage for their young adulthood when your hands will gradually release your hold on their futures.

Becoming Young Adults: Adolescence

As your children move into their teens, you will observe rapid weight gains and sometimes outlandish appetites. This is not to suggest that they will be overweight, *although it is important that you guard against that,* but that they will fill out into the full flesh and musculature of young adults.

Nourishing food in appropriate amounts and elimination of snacking will help you build strong young people of appropriate size and weight. We repeat, make clear to them that you recognize their greater need for food, yet help them not to lean on food as an emotional crutch and end up obese and poorly adjusted. You do not want them to get caught, as so many do, in a desperate cycle, which sees their emotional torments calling for more food and their obesity reducing the self-respect they need to deal with their personal doubts.

Boys are now catching up and passing girls in height, but not yet in judgment nor emotional maturity, although they have usually caught up with the girls in coordination and in ability to reason and learn. Unfortunately, because of early formal school at a time of immaturity, many more boys will have difficulty with studies. By secondary school there will be at least eight boys to every girl in classes for the emotionally impaired and thirteen to every girl in therapy for the learning disabled.[1]

Your teenagers will reach adult height and will essentially complete their bone growth. Now they become mature in sexual ability, with girls moving gradually two to three years ahead of boys, including both physical and emotional changes. In this process the glands are also developing and may at first be out of balance. Their hearts are growing rapidly in order to support their overall development.

You should be aware of their tendencies to think they know it all, with some emotional instability and temptation to go to extremes. If they have been reared with their peers more than with their parents, you may be certain that in dress, diet, deportment, and recreation they will be heavily influenced by agemates, however extreme or conservative the culture. Still they have an underlying ethical curiosity and an interest in philosophical and religious ideas and in the possibility of a future life. They are far deeper and more altruistic in their thinking than most parents believe, but the peer, and sometimes parental, pressures can stifle such ideals at a time when they are searching for and need them most.

More than ever teenagers want acceptance by their social groups. Yet those who have been taught longer at home before entering conventional schools are far more likely to be comfortable with you and other adults and with little children as well as with their peers. They do have a natural fear of ridicule as they turn from children to adults and tend to be oversensitive. Self-pity often emerges and can best be discouraged by getting their minds on the needs of others and on constructive work. Sports, with all their ego risks, are seldom good medicine for such self-concern.

Both boys and girls have a strong interest in physical attractiveness, although their standards for perfection may be far from yours. Be patient. Although they feel their need to assert their independence from you and your family, one of their most impelling needs is for identification with a strong adult figure. If fathers have been close to their daughters during their earlier years, their daughters will be looking up to them now. While sons also need their fathers as male models, they can learn much of tenderness and affection from a warm and responsive mother.

Adolescents have many needs as they move into full maturity. First of all, they may not be fully aware of the nearing likelihood of heading families. Now is the time to insure that your children have at least one manual skill by which they can earn a living, and give them opportunities to earn and to save, in which they share the decision making. Both boys and girls should have some understanding of cooking and nutrition, hygiene, physiology, and safety. They must learn how to work dependably. They must learn that one day their security will be their own responsibility. This lesson has been harder to come by since World War II, for parents have been more and more preoccupied with other things and have given little attention to the work ethic for their children.

As they think of future responsibilities, don't fail to teach them by precept and example that no man is a real man who does not take tender care of his wife and family. If he is to be the family leader, he must deserve it by going over halfway in patience, kindness, forgiveness, and thoughtfulness of others. This is especially well taught at this idealistic age. Boys should be willing to share in the housework and learn that it will stand them in good stead when they need to lend a hand.

Likewise girls should remember that their femininity is among their most prized possessions. The feminine nature is better demonstrated in kindness to others and tenderness to their husbands and families than in competing with the Joneses in life-styles. To be frugal, manage well, prepare nutritious food, and even make and patch clothes is more to be desired than to be a society leader.

It is important for both boys and girls to have sound information and understanding of sexual relationships and standards.[2] Patience with one another in early friendships and during courtship will pay big dividends later. Above all developmental eras, now is the time to sacrifice present pleasures for future benefits. Let them know that if they want genuine self-respect and the respect of their future partners, if they want that winsome and exciting experience of the best of honeymoons, now is the time to build self-control.

Now is also the time to be unobtrusive in your interest in their affairs, yet alert to their developmental needs and ready to do your share. Let them be independent as far as they can accept the responsibility. At the same time allow them the privilege of being dependent, so long as they don't demand that you indulge them.

By the time your children have reached this age, you will be keenly aware that your practice of understanding of their development, combined with commonsense and affection, will be an exercise in self-control, both for them and for you. Such self-discipline is the fine art of discipleship, which is the open door to leadership.

If you have been consistent in your example, treatment, and instruction of your children, they will now have become quite capable of making good choices of behavior, especially if you remain their most loyal companions and friends. Peer relationships are important to them, but they will be independent thinkers if their elective time has been more with you than with their friends and if your times and counsel are easily available for their needs. Children, even into and through their adult years, should be willing to seek counsel from you and other adults. Also, as long as they live in your house, they must know, respect, and abide by your standards. In their teen years they often will look to you to help them in dealing with different peer situations.

One time a friend of our son Dennis offered him a ride on

his motorcycle after school. Dennis was already something of an expert in cycling up the mountain trails around our home, although he stayed away from highways at our request. Dorothy was really uncomfortable with the idea of his riding with this boy. Now here was a test: she was there to take him home in our car. She said to Dennis, "I think it would be better if you came home with me."

When they got into the car, Dennis said, "Mother, I'm glad you said what you did. I really didn't want to go with him, but I didn't know how to get out of it." There comes a time when parents must be strong enough in their maturity to insist on principle even at the risk of not being liked. Handled with loving firmness this brings discipleship to our children.

PART THREE

TEN BUILDING BLOCKS
OF
COMMONSENSE DISCIPLINE

9
Warm Responsiveness and Example

I was running down the slopes of Mount Ararat in 1964 with a member of the Turkish Olympic Ski Team when suddenly we came upon a giant gray wolf that was concentrating so intensely on something down the mountain that he was entirely unaware of us. Looking down to the right, we saw a little reddish-brown lamb. There is nothing a Turkish wolf likes better than a fresh leg of lamb, and this lamb was about to meet a big bad wolf! He had strayed from the flock, and neither the shepherd nor his dog knew it.

Whether it be a mature sheep or goat or a lamb or a kid, danger lingers always on the side of that mountain. I was struck almost instantly with the lesson in that picture and with how often I had let other things preoccupy me when I should have been closer to my "kids." In that Kurdish country the tribesmen so value their sheep that they treat them much like their children: they make sure always that someone is sleeping at the gate of the fold. In fact they are the gate of the fold. These men are close to their families; their children share the pastures with them. Responsiveness and warmth are the name of their family game.

Such parents are not slaves to their children; they are affectionate, but firm, guides. While living among them I never heard fathers or mothers raise their voices at their children. When children misbehaved, there seemed to be a deliberate wait before parents addressed the problem—no passionate words, but a time of silence that is golden.

The silence could of course be ominous, but whatever the

result, that period did give the children a chance to think—something that children seldom have time for nowadays. The children were not provoked to anger because of an unreasonable action of their parent; they were secure in the certainty that whatever response came would be just.

Yet there did seem to be one impulsive practice among these mountain people: they grinned and applauded every good thing their children did. Such warmth and gratitude was the underwriting of a discipleship training that put punishment in perspective when that did become necessary. Thus, day by day the children learned lessons for future usefulness, cradled in warm and responsive hearts.

In 1960 *Horizon* magazine published the Smithsonian Institution report on the development of genius, authored by North Carolina University psychologist, Harold McCurdy, who studied characteristics of great geniuses and leaders through the ages. The Smithsonian recipe for genius includes (1) "a high degree of attention focused upon the child by parents and other adults, expressed in intensive educational measures and, usually, abundant love"; (2) isolation from other children, especially outside the family; and (3) free exploration under parental guidance (in the sand pile, in encyclopedias, in scientific experiments, in music, arts, history, social service) instead of slavery to adult imagination.[1] The parental example and response reign as constructive and preventive influences in family discipline.

Your Example—the Best Control

Getting your own life in order as a parent is the first step in rearing well-behaved children. Start with the simple things: making a start on getting organized by developing a schedule that multiplies your time and effectiveness; living within your means; and planning constructive things for and with your children at very young ages.

A father with grown children confided to us that he had not lived the kind of self-disciplined life he had wanted his children to develop. He had sent them to private schools, to Boy Scouts, and even to church to make sure they were taught high moral and behavior values. He *upheld* his wife in her ideals, yet never modeled them himself. In grief he told us that "What I was spoke louder than what I said."

One father headed off in the snow for work one morning, planning as usual to stop at a nearby café for a beer. As he plodded along he sensed that someone was behind him. He turned to look and saw his little boy with oversize steps, trying to match his footsteps and heard, "Me coming, Daddy. Me yite in oo twacks."

Children learn by observation and imitation. Adults who exemplify the right characteristics and who care enough for the child to help him attain the desired qualities provide the ideal role models. Contrariwise, other young children who are themselves not carriers of sound ethical values simply help to multiply their weaknesses as they associate with your children or other peers. Take special pains to build sound behavior in your first child, for he or she will be a role model for your subsequent children.

Treat your children with courtesy and respect if you want them to be courteous and respectful. For example, if you are interested in teaching your child courtesy as well as helping him develop concentration (a long attention span), do not interrupt his play unnecessarily or abruptly. Play is to children what work is to adults, and most often their play copies adults' work.

Try this for a standard behavior problem: if you want them to learn to chew with their mouths closed, take time to discuss it *when the family is alone* together or even with the child alone. Demonstrate the difference—with something crunchy like celery, crisp toast, or crackers. When others are around,

107

whisper a reminder if necessary. Such gentle reminders avoid embarrassment for children (in contrast to a public reprimand) and elicit warm cooperation.

Possibly the greatest of all robberies in modern history is de- priving our children of the three crucial ingredients (adult re- sponses, isolation from other children, and opportunity for free exploration) by pushing them early out of home, where they could have an average of a hundred to three hundred responses from their parents daily—compared to one to three a day at school. These crimes against our offspring are con- summated under the influence of the state and so-called pro- fessionals who in fact are specialists in pursuing their vested interests—jobs, dollars, influence, and other "professional perquisites" with little concern for children.

The Most Pervasive Child Abuse

But perhaps the most criminal influence of all is the parent who happily gives in to these conventional trends simply be- cause everybody else is doing it. Social pressure dictates it, and who wants to defy public opinion?

No wonder we have so many abortions today. They are popular, even status symbols among some groups. How about rapes? In some gangs, rape is one of the requirements for good standing. The principle is precisely the same whether we are discussing rape or getting rid of our children, which is sim- ply rape of another kind—of their young minds and spirits.

I believe that such rape includes institutionalizing these pre- cious charges of ours unnecessarily in day-care facilities and preschools, where they receive only a few adult responses a day at most, and sometimes no dialogue at all. This is not only true in franchised day care, but also in public schools, where a 1983 study found that the average teacher spends about seven minutes of the school day in personal exchanges with students.[2] Classrooms are so cluttered these days with educa- tional litter—reports, films, extra-curricular activities, and so forth—that teachers do not have time for the personal touch that builds genius and character.

When you are building great character in your children, you might consider which house can better stand in a storm: one that was built deliberately with careful planning—on concrete that was dry, with wood that was well seasoned, and all finished out with loving care—or one that was built in a rush—on uncured concrete, with green, warping wood, by speculators in a hurry. *It never pays to rush children.*

Some excuse themselves by justifying their "quality" time as superior to "quantity" time. Indeed a parent can be at home with a child all day and not be responsive—providing neither quality nor quantity care. Children do not develop or learn in concentrated doses. They need continuing assurance that comfort, security, answers to questions, and other needs are available from a loving parent most of the time. On the other hand, a child should not be allowed to be demanding of a parent but should learn as soon as possible a cooperative relationship of give and take. As we said earlier, children should learn that household duties are theirs to share, and care of their siblings is a privilege.

There are, of course, families whose children must have early out-of-home care because of single parenthood or financial distress or illness. These children should receive family-like care—from qualified relatives or friends (family day care) or similar sources—until school age instead of being burned out in formal programs at early ages. But this is no excuse for the rest of us.

Several years ago I was visiting a preschool that was said to be the best preschool in Paris, France, located a block or two from UNESCO, which is supposed to be the international headquarters for education and culture. One sweet, young teacher had twenty-two two-and-a-half-year-olds in the morning and another twenty-one children each afternoon. Few of them were really potty trained, and some were still in diapers.

But that is the pattern for the *Écoles maternelle* ("mothering schools") in France, which enroll over 99 percent of that nation's children at this early age. The sweet mademoiselle said to me, "Oh, Dr. Moore, if I could only have them two or three at a time in my apartment!" She, like many thoughtful teachers, knew and loved her children.

Yet, that is the very specter just ahead for America if she kowtows to such power plays as the National Education Association's demand for school for all by age three or four. Psychiatrist John Bowlby of the World Health Organization suggests that it is an even worse form of child abuse than the alcoholic father who hits his child, since the child of the alcoholic father knows he has a home.

Smithsonian author Harold McCurdy concluded that "the mass education of our public school system is, in its way, a vast experiment on the effect of reducing all three factors [adult responses, isolation from other children, opportunity for exploration] to a minimum; accordingly, it should tend to suppress the occurrence of genius."[3] Certainly this is also the modern school's record on discipline. Dr. McCurdy's recipe is a commonsense reason for not rushing little children into school and is totally compatible with nearly all replicated research on school entrance.

Parent and teacher response, along with example, is a most powerful educational tool and is one of the best guarantors of sound discipline. When that response is warm and consistent and when it is reasonably patient, the parent or teacher usually receives immediate warmth in return.

We do not suggest that parents and teachers go overboard in making talk, but that they be alert always to child or student needs, including tentative requests for help and actual questions or appeals. Otherwise, more often than not, we are likely to be so preoccupied with other cares that we fail to respond, and before long such indifference becomes a habit. The instinctive and logical childish reaction is, "If they don't care enough to answer me, I will ignore them, too." And shortly they seek their information from sources of which you may not approve.

Responses are not necessarily verbal. Some demand very little talk. A pat on the shoulder, a squeeze of a hand, a hug, or a kiss on the forehead or cheek says volumes to a youngster who is trying hard to do a good job at home, at school, or at work. Cautions are in order where there is a crossing of the sexes, as for example a man who is responding to his step-daughter, a man or woman teacher or even an uncle or an aunt who is working with a student or relative of the opposite sex. Your motive and your commonsense will clearly distinguish between appropriate affection and lust. If there is any of the latter, keep hands off!

A short, hand-written note, now and then, can be a treasure for the recipient and a valuable tool of preventive discipline. Gentle, encouraging words are always appropriate for relationships which are not blood-linked and for some which are. They will be filled with thought and will bring out the best in those they seek to help.

111

Routine, Regularity, and Order

As I mentioned earlier, it took me some twenty years of marriage to realize that it was my business to see that things were picked up and not leave them all to my wife. Still another ten years went by before I refined the organization of my closet. Why I didn't do it before is a measure of my thoughtlessness, but I had to learn, since I was asking Dorothy to help me in my work and she was doing it *more* than full-time.

Now I hang all the shirts and suits in my closet in the same direction. Shirts, jackets, and suits hang in groups. Blue shirts are together, white ones likewise, ranging from dark down to light. All shirts that have been used but are not yet dirty enough to launder hang at the front of the shirt section. The same is true of shoes and suits and ties and belts—a place for everything and everything in its place.

It hasn't always been that easy. For six months during one of our tours in Washington, D.C., after the children were grown, Dorothy and I lived in an attic bedroom and shared a bathroom and kitchen with the owners of the house. We managed on one large closet. For drawers we used cardboard boxes, neatly cut. And to save my wife from prostration, we cut back on every unnecessary chore.

We all do better with a reasonable amount of structure in our lives because of our natural body rhythms, but infants and small children particularly are creatures of routine. Nearly all children up through the early teens find security in regularity at home. In their younger years you must plan the program, lay down the rules, and see that they are consistently followed. Consistency is a jewel in discipline. As your children grow older, they may be brought into the planning and also into the enforcement of the rules.

Give your youngsters reasons for your actions when they show an aptness for reasoning; take them into your confidence. Make sure that your reasoning is logical. For example, in setting bedtime hours, world specialists in circadian (body) rhythms declare that the hours before midnight are two or three times as valuable for sleep as the morning hours. Thus, "Early to bed, early to rise" can become a healthy and happy reality. The family is up without rush, can have breakfast together, and then can see father off to work.

We know many families who have a short morning story-time before Daddy leaves and evening story hours after he returns. A treasured side effect of such routines is a collection of family traditions—precious memories children often cherish for life and sometimes pass on to their children. For example, when we lived in Japan we always had a favorite rice dish called *O-sushi* for supper on Friday nights. Also since we lived in a rather poorly heated house, we all sat close together on the sofa with a fluffy, soft robe over our laps and legs for evening storytime.

Any daily, weekly, or holiday routines can become powerful agents to cement families together and establish family loyalty as well as bring highly effective preventive discipline. Normal children will accept discipline as they experience the affection and closeness of their family.

Meals likewise should be regular. Rooms should be picked up and straightened daily and cleaned as often as is reasonable by the children—or at least with their assistance—from the time they begin to walk. Closets should be kept in order, toys and books in their assigned places, even if they are cardboard boxes.

Your goal is to make yourself and your children uncomfortable when their clothes, shoes, toys, and books are littered around the house. With your example and consistency, this will not take long to establish. Such self-discipline is discipline's highest goal.

Regularity

Regularity should be the rule in most aspects of family life. Regular schedules, within reasonable bounds, should be set for chores, play, meals, and rest. Yet don't feel so frozen to your program that your conscience plagues you if you take time out or make an occasional exception. A frustrated mother apologetically wrote to Dorothy:

I'm a little uncomfortable about imposing on you for advice, but I am having a problem with my six-year-old son. He was potty trained at two years. There was no power struggle—and yet he still messes his pants. He's done it off and on since he was three, and lately it's been constant.

I talked to his doctor about it a year ago, and he made such a big deal about it in front of Jimmy, I felt it would only cause it to become a bigger problem in Jimmy's mind if I discussed it any more. I've tried rewards for cleanliness, explaining the reason we have b.m.'s—digestive system—how he smells bad, etc. He doesn't have a bowel movement in his pants, but he doesn't want to take time and go, so he just "messes."

Now, each time I notice, I'm having him wash out his own underwear, shower, and do a load of wash with his undies included. It doesn't seem to affect him at all! I don't sense it is proper to spank for this. I love him dearly and feel I'm letting him down by not knowing how I should deal with this.

Dorothy thought that was a pretty big order, but she tackled it the best she could with the following letter:

114

I wish I could talk with you so I could explain things a little bit better. But one of the first things I would do is to see that he is on a *very regular schedule*. You might even have to go almost to the extreme on this in terms of *regular* meals, *regular* bedtime, and *regular* everything as much as possible.

One of the routines I would instigate would be a pint of warm water a half hour before breakfast. This flushes the kidneys, prepares the digestive system for breakfast, tones the bowels, and encourages peristalsis.

Then I would give him a fresh orange and a fresh apple for breakfast, along with cereal or eggs or whatever else you have. Immediately after breakfast I would have him sit on the toilet. Give him a book or something so that he can be happy about it. But he should sit there up to a half hour, not necessarily straining but making some kind of effort to move his bowels. In other words, you are going to try to train him at this somewhat late date to form the habit of a regular bowel movement before or *immediately after breakfast every day*.

Include a great many fresh fruits and vegetables in his diet and eliminate all constipating foods, such as white bread or sweets of any kind. If he has whole grains, lots of fruits and vegetables, and plenty of water between meals (at least four additional glasses of water not close to meals), he should become regular soon because everything else is regular.

The only discipline involved should be in carefully and tenderly applying these three principles of proper diet, water, and regularity in your everyday routine. What he is doing now is not only a hygienic problem, but it also can lead to constipation because resisting the urge can bring this on and then a train of other ills.

You might be interested to know that I initially bowel-trained my children in this way and this habit has remained with them to this day. Such a habit is not only a matter of hygiene, but also a matter of health.

Less than two weeks later Betty wrote back to Dorothy. Betty's response was a surprise, since Dorothy did not expect the results to come so fast. Betty's insights in terms of her own self-discipline were especially gratifying to Dorothy because that indeed is the bottom line. Here are excerpts from her letter:

I just wanted to write you a note and let you know how well Jimmy is doing. After following your advice—the results have been amazing. He has had a bowel movement every morning from the first day I implemented this schedule and has not had any messy pants at all. The boys balk a little at a pint of tepid water before breakfast, but actually they've been very agreeable. . . .

Dorothy, I want to thank you sincerely for your time and help. It pleases me so much to mature in self-discipline and to be able to model this before my children—teaching them the value of this important quality. Yet usually I do not have access to people who have clearly thought out these "preventive medicine" types of discipline. The brilliance and simplicity of these concepts amaze me—teaching through scheduling and a prepared environment that reinforces the values we hold dear. It also teaches parents self-control and a confidence in parenting that is so lacking.

Order

Every home is not alike, so we do not lay down detailed rules on cleanliness and order. Yet principles are universal. There is no excuse for sloppiness and filth, not even for most of those in poverty. In the days of the Great Depression the Moores knew poverty, but our standard of cleanliness and order did not suffer; Dad insisted that we have self-respect. He knew that few things destroy it more completely than personal carelessness.

Although sometimes children may not seem to like it, they are in a sense creatures of order as well as of routine. They feel much more secure when there is an orderly program. Those of you who have moved often know this well. The silverware is in a different drawer, the closets are smaller or shaped differently, there is no broom closet, and the bed is now in the corner and harder to make.

The hippies and the youth rebellion of the 1960s, whatever else they brought us good or bad, did breed a carelessness, a recklessness about personal grooming and cleanness and order, which infected our entire society. A distaste for neatness and order seemed to prevail, whether it involved clothes, hair, bedrooms, or the mind. The indifference to good taste and respect for order reached even into churches and synagogues. The aftermath of war and its parental preoccupation with materialism probably was responsible for this unmannered generation.

Although many of those youth, now adults, have mended their ways, mature and gentle people often wonder at the indifference and disrespect commonly shown to older adults, a startling example of disorderliness of the mind. This has been passed on to our children today, who often ignore even common courtesies and who call their elders by their first names with little more respect for them and their long experience than they have for an adolescent or a pet dog. The random littering—from cigarette butts and beer cans to loads of junk— is a sign of disordered minds. Parents and teachers like you and me can do a lot toward bringing manners and self-worth back home and making the Golden Rule shine again.

The sum of the man is in his self-worth, whether he is a Christian, Moslem, or Jew. There is seldom any excuse for disorder of the environment or the mind. Whether rich or poor, educated or unschooled, we can always find a way to make do if we are convinced that our example and our comfort is worth the cost.

Constructive Work and Play

I n California's Regional Occupational Programs (ROPs) public schools have found that when half the school day is devoted to work, the students excel in both achievement and behavior—even though the work is done without pay. Such is the record of work programs around the world at all levels of education.

Home schools across America are finding that afternoons spent on family industries are exciting to both children and adults. Many children are delighted at making five cents an hour selling lemonade. Others earn up to $50 a day selling muffins, sandwiches, or other goods and services. Some mothers with their children bring in as much as $150 on the days they clean homes or apartments. Outdoor work is as appropriate as indoor work for mothers and fathers with their sons and daughters.

There is no greater active force for sound discipline than manual work. Busy children are less likely to cause parents stress. Properly carried out and especially *when you work with your children,* work becomes a genuine blessing, and children come to enjoy it at least as much as play. Until adults help them know the difference, children love work.

Josh, a typical four-year-old early riser, comes to his daddy's bedside, gently pats him on the face, and whispers, "Daddy, let's go play in the garden." This daddy, who is also an early riser, delights to go and "play" with Josh in a mid-city garden. Yet this is not a putdown on play—which children

118

need primarily to develop their imaginations and creative abilities and to exercise their large muscles.

Work

Work is a crucially important activity for the highest form of discipline, both preventive and remedial. And as they build brain, bone, and muscle, children will require far less of the pleasure-amusement exercise which preoccupies most of our children today and hardly builds character like manual work *with you*.

William James, the great Harvard philosopher, was once asked, "If you could choose, what would be the one most important activity you would prescribe for school children?" He replied that he would "increase enormously the amount of manual or 'motor' training relatively to the book-work, and not let the latter preponderate until the age of 15 or 16."[1] This counsel fits well with that of top learning psychologists such as University of California's William Rohwer, who would prefer that children wait for formal schooling until junior high school ages, in which event millions of school children who are doomed to failure under the traditional education system could have academic success.[2]

Sound work habits lead not only to self-worth and free enterprise, but also to neatness, order, cleanliness, integrity, dependability, nobility of character, and even purity of thought. Minds and hands work together constructively instead of using time for indulgent amusements. When children involve the larger muscles in a sound exercise program, they also tend to insure sounder sleep.

As early as possible, help your child to enjoy solitude some of the time. Even an infant will learn to explore his own hands, feet, or toys in or near his bed if you do not run to him at every fuss or cry. This in no way suggests neglect or scarcity of time with you and the family, but when you provide constant entertainment and attention, you may make your child demanding and incapable of being happy and occupied by himself.

Children not only can share work chores, but can be involved in free enterprise from very early years and continue this activity with surprising results through their teenage years or until they leave home. Near Niles, Michigan, not long ago, a five- and six-year-old boy and girl sold lemonade in the summer for ten cents a glass at their roadside apple-box store. Nearby, from another box they sold tomatoes out of a garden "we weeded ourselves." A neat, adult-lettered sign laid down an integrity challenge to prospective clients—"ON YOUR HONOR"—in deference to the youngsters' immature arithmetic ability.

In Grants Pass, Oregon, we learned, as we were finishing this book, that Henry and Robin Martin had thought twice about their children, Heidi, then fifteen, and Brent, eleven, in view of the many distractions these days. They have family worship and otherwise try to set a sound example for their offspring, yet they felt they had to do more. They considered employing the youngsters in their prosperous Mercedes-Volvo-Nissan dealership, but decided on a better course: they conferred with Heidi and Brent about starting their own business. Parental guidance would, of course, be provided in a businesslike way, but without interfering unduly with personal initiative. Peer pressures were soon forgotten as Brent began selling vegetables from his garden and Heidi made whole wheat bread and later delicious muffins from which, at last accounting, she was grossing about $60 a day, with a very neat profit.

The Martins gather at evening mealtime or before or after family worship when Heidi and Brent give an accounting for the day. Some of these are quite exciting times as they discuss experiences with people as well as money and make corrections in plans and practice where necessary. Careful but simple books are kept so that the young merchandisers know exactly where they stand. They have learned that parental guidance is not parental interference.

Remedial discipline—punishment—is seldom if ever necessary in the Martin home because Mother and Dad practice the highest order of constructive and preventive discipline through work experience—hands-on business lessons. And incidentally, Heidi and Brent are learning some very practical mathematics, economics, and personal and public relations.

Occasionally such kids sell personal property and real estate, or actually manufacture. In New Orleans, Andreas Anderson, then age fourteen, began making computer ROMs. The last I talked with him he estimated his income on "a few hours a week, at about $50 an hour." These industries far excel formal studies for building sound citizens. Families plan together, with children participating as officers of the family corporation and helping, when necessary, to manage the money. This may be the most effective of all remedies for burned-out children or for behavior problems. Interestingly enough, these enterprising parents often are not in financial need, but do this for the fun of building their children.[3]

In most families children who have become thus involved have become neighborhood leaders, as, for example, all those mentioned above. In many homes these children employ neighborhood friends, and usually such homes are well-ordered social centers of their areas. The most successful programs, we stress, enjoy active parent encouragement and participation where necessary and wanted.

Play

Play has its place, too. The reason we do not emphasize it more is that most of it is already overemphasized and badly directed. Children are over-toyed, over-entertained, and over-amused at home, at school, and wherever they go. Give your children a chance to develop concentration and coordination as well as creativity in play, and you will discover a new spirit in them.

Give them a simple sandbox on the porch or in the yard. During cold weather bring the sand inside your house or garage in a large tub or plastic wading pool. Or give them tools instead of toys and watch them enjoy longer those toys they make themselves, with a great deal less expense than the shiny pieces bought from the local store, which are soon stacked up in their closets or are littering the yard. One example is a hammer and short strong nails and pieces of scrap wood, which you can easily scavenge from a lumber company or construction site.

If you want a balanced, well-disciplined family, we offer an additional suggestion which will be hard for some families to accept, and I speak as a former public school coach who graduated from the University of Southern California. Yet it is one of the most important of all: Avoid *rivalry* sports. They very seldom build the selfless, pioneering spirit on which our nation was founded, and they offer a poor substitute for the work ethic, which we now largely ignore.

Many parents get excited at the possibilities of Little League for children between the ages of six to eight. They are not ready for the rivalry that normally prevails. This is the very time when you should be doing all you can to socialize your children in a *positive* way instead of supporting their naturally selfish instincts. Little League types of recreation make home discipline much more difficult, often raise impossible expectations of children, and create disharmony between parent and child as parents turn on the pressure, often out of vanity instead of parental concern for their children.

However, we do not necessarily condemn sports in which there is simple competition, as long as sports do not take priority over chores and other constructive work. We have had particular success when members of the teams are exchanged during the game—as rotating around the net in volleyball or exchanging one team member each inning in baseball.

Business competition is often offered as an excuse for encouraging competition among young children. Yet the best of businessmen accentuate cooperation as well as competition. I remember well inquiring for a certain tire from a local tire store, only to find that the right tire was not in stock. I was referred to a competitor who stocked the same brand and happened to have the right size. This is desirable competition, not selfish rivalry, yet this is seldom the way with rivalry sports.

Few children can handle genuine rivalry with all of its "me-first" overtones until they are capable of mature reasoning, which for most children is around ages eleven or twelve. Even then, few if any, really profit by it. Even worse, most sports today are for most people spectator sports; few actively participate. For most they are passive amusements which damage health and certainly discourage that self-control which should be discipline's goal.

Service to Others

I remember well how our dad, a successful and busy head of his own business and a widower, would take us three little kids to the Old Soldier's home at Sawtelle in Southern California. This was not a happenstance, but a regular, carefully planned weekend trip across town for us. Dad would invite some of our favorite playmates along, until he had a troupe of several families visiting those old heroes weekly. We would take them carefully selected papers and magazines, but they would wait until after we left before reading them. And, boy, did the old gentlemen like us!

We got far more than our share of hugs and pats from men who sometimes did not have another visitor all week. We felt needed, appreciated, and genuinely loved by those veterans. We somehow sensed that they depended on us, and we did not want to disappoint them. Service to others increases our intrinsic self-worth like magic—no pretense, no grouching. We just enjoyed seeing their eyes light up. The law of self-serving is the law of self-destruction, but the vision of service is eternal. Through all the ages, surviving societies are those which, no matter how hungry, always saved their seed grain. They gave to multiply. So it is with the spirit of service; it is the ultimate joy. This is true in the world, in the nation, in the community, and in the school, but above all, it reaches its zenith in marriage and in the family: father taking care of mother, mother standing at his side, caring parents living close to their kids. On the other hand, if we do not learn and do not teach our children to serve, we become slaves to our own indulgences and eventually to a despot who does not care.

Even with these verified lessons of history, America (and the Western world) has moved from the country to the city; it has largely discarded the work ethic in education simply by change of life-style from raising its own food to the cramped urban environments where providing such constructive chores is not always easy. We have become indulgers and entertainers of men and women instead of builders, when we have easily within our reach a jewel of great price for both prevention and remedy of dependency and delinquency! The jewel is the spirit of service—to the community, state, nation, and world; to poor, needy, ill, aged, and imprisoned; to neighbors and friends and, occasionally, to someone who has done us wrong.

We have watched the excitement as children have substituted gift-giving for trick-or-treating on Halloween. We have observed the genuine dignity of candy-stripers as they serve in hospitals across the nation. We have witnessed high school students of California's Regional Occupation Programs cleaning up parks and streets, and with great admiration we have watched church youth groups cleaning litter from Maryland, Michigan, California, and Washington highways.

You will seldom find delinquency issuing from such programs. These children generate self-worth and respect for their neighbors and their town. In the process they build personal standards, which qualify them as better citizens and community leaders. Start your own program in your home; then expand it to your neighbors of your choice whose children will make good companions in service. The service motive, carefully nurtured, will save you hours and years of strain by creating a constructive base for rearing your children.

Most child psychologists that we know agree on at least one thing: Self-worth is the greatest, and perhaps the most important, single need for your children. And clinical psychologists and psychiatrists have similar views for adults. In such service both you and your children can find such fulfillment. We remind you several times in this book that self-worth is much more than *self-esteem* as it is commonly conceived, for it is the fruit of the Golden Rule. There are poise and power in self-worth and self-respect while the word *self-esteem* often carries with it anything but selflessness—the very quality which the service principle builds so well.

When I was a university officer in Southern California, we were reminded from time to time that our children received more than average scrutiny. Yet they had the same temptations that were causing many teenagers to stumble. So we got together with several other families in the community, including physicians from the university's medical center, in a search for something constructive for our children to do, and we took the youngsters into our planning.

We organized a program essentially run by the students, which they nicknamed "S.O.S."—which stood for a number of things relating to service. We met on Saturday nights at light, informal, fruit-salad-and-popcorn parties and planned for the next week. The projects ranged from fixing furniture and washing machines to cleaning houses, pulling weeds, and preparing gardens—all for the ill or needy, and nearly all without the recipients knowing who did it. Sometimes the young people had to contact neighbors, relatives, or even the police to be sure that their work was not mistaken for breaking and entering. To this day, twenty-five years later, they remain excited about those episodes. Our S.O.S. club did save our "ships"—our youngsters—as we were helping to save others.

There are a few true extroverts (which means "an individual interested in others," rather than someone who is outgoing) in the world, and you will almost invariably find that they are involved in selfless service to their families and neighbors. They are so rare that sometimes they are considered unconventional, and they take the risk that they may be thought dated or strange. Yet ultimately, whatever their religion or absence of claimed religion, they are the world's only really happy people.

·················· **13** ··················
Camaraderie, Courtesy, and Communication

My left thumb carries a long scar, running diagonally from below the knuckle down toward my hand. It is a souvenir from my experiment in short-cutting my father's instruction to pull a patch of weeds on the west side of our Richmond, California, home. The area was no more than six feet square, but to a six-year-old boy it looked like an acre. So I sneaked out Grandma's butcher knife and began hacking away the weeds, holding a bundle of them at the top while I tried to cut near the roots. On one of those swipes, I missed!

That was the only occasion I can recall when Dad did not work with me on a "major" project. I don't think he had any idea how big that weed patch looked to me. As Charles and I grew into preteens and adolescence, Dad brought us often to his jobs and taught us reinforced concrete construction and cement finishing, how to build houses and stores and to pave sidewalks and roads and tennis courts. Always he worked *with* us or gave us responsibility which kept us on the stretch while he was gone, until by age sixteen he had us running his crews. Working with him was the greatest educational experience of my young life.

From the time your children start to walk, work with them, even if it is only putting toys away. As they grow, you will give them independent things to do, such as making the bed and shining their own shoes; eventually they can pick up after you instead of you always bending over! During their early years you will make great gains when they participate in the simplest activities. Then you will graduate them to washing the dishes and the car *with* you and mowing the lawn—jobs which in due time they will proudly take over by themselves. Keep challenging them to grow into new and larger responsibilities.

But working with them is not enough. You will want to play with them, camp with them, visit them occasionally in their classes at church or in school, or in other out-of-home activities such as 4-H and Scouts. No matter what the projects may be, make it your high priority to be involved. Too many parents allow other people or institutions, though well-meaning and often efficient, to do their parenting for them. Scoutmasters, 4-H directors and sport coaches can never fully take your place.

Be sure to listen to them—a skill which few parents cultivate, but if learned well, listening will give you a running start in your discipline. Adults are considered sources of information, but children also need to express their feelings, fears, ideas, and attitudes to them.

Some time ago, we were waiting for a plane at O'Hare Field in Chicago when we noticed a boy about six years old calling his father's attention to some loading activity outside the gate. Apparently their baggage was going up the conveyor belt into their plane. They were obviously a well-to-do family, judging from their clothes, the mother's leather accessories, their daughter's designer clothes, the way the two boys were dressed, and their first-class boarding passes for the flight to Hawaii.

"Daddy, Daddy," the little boy called from the window over by gate F-3.

No answer. His father was deep in the sports section of the Sunday *Chicago Tribune*.

"Daddy, look!" he urged. "Our baggage!"

Still no answer, although his mother looked up momentarily, and his brother and sister quickly joined him at the window.

Again the boy called, "Daddy, *our* baggage," this time racing over to where his father was sitting and poking him lightly on the shoulder.

"Huh?" was the father's response.

"I wantcha to see our stuff goin' into our plane. . . ."

"Never mind," called his big brother. "It's already gone."

"Oh, I've seen that many times," his father finally spoke.

The youngster's disappointment was obvious, and his mother murmured, "Daddy is tired, you know."

"He's always tired," was the boy's wearied response, as both his father and mother missed a genuine opportunity to express the parental interest and camaraderie every child needs. Camaraderie and communication in the early years help to guarantee accessibility and loyalty in the crucial teen years. A study out of the University of North Carolina strongly asserts that the deteriorating bond between parents and children is responsible for the most serious problems of adolescent youths. In the past such results were blamed on economic, social, or ethnic conditions—an all-purpose explanation often used by social scientists to place blame. However, during the time frame of this study, all these usually considered relevant conditions dramatically improved, thus laying the responsibility on the particular individuals concerned. Two-thirds of parents surveyed felt that they should have the freedom to live their own lives even if it meant spending less time with their children.[1]

In contrast, we recently watched the Laurito family welcome their daddy back home at their row house in Philadelphia. He is a city policeman and was obviously worn out after doing some overtime on the beat. Yet he embraced every one of the five children, tossing the smaller ones into the air and giving special tenderness to the little black baby they were keeping for a teenaged mother. Although their mother was teaching all five at home, through age fourteen, their home was the social center of the neighborhood. And judging from the examples of their warm and responsive parents, it was not difficult to understand why.

If you look your children in the eye when you talk with them and they learn to do the same, you will not have much trouble with their listening to you. This is an especially valuable technique when you want to impress them, such as when you are giving important instructions. I think of one mother who made a special point of this with her daughter, who would otherwise have been more forgetful and difficult to control. We do not speak of staring them down. This is never a way to make friends. But eye-to-eye contact at anytime, whether for appreciation or remonstrance, has power that you cannot possibly exert without it. Unfortunately, too often this power is used when you are displeased, but it has its greatest force when used to express pleasure.

Wait your children out, no matter how silly, boring, or unnecessary their talk may seem. They are a part of the family tree, one of your branches. Treat them with consideration if you want your tree to look good and bear the right kind of fruit.

As you move along with your children in their development, you will find that they will have fun being with you if you are excited about being with them. Thousands of parents are joining their children, not only in play, but in visiting the sick and needy in their neighborhoods, as the Lauritos did. Or in setting up a family business with you. Let them be officers, let them have their own cards, and plan *with* you, as we have observed elsewhere in this volume.

Your warmth and responsiveness are the roots of genius and stability, and your selflessness with them will be the wellspring of a well-mannered family. They will behave well around others when they see you at your best in your social circles, for they already have seen you practice what you preach at home. Whether at a restaurant, at a party, or at

131

church, they will delight in reflecting credit upon you if you have delighted in them enough to demonstrate good taste and concern for others in your personal lives with them.

If you want to have some real fun, ask your librarian for a good book on manners, and take turns playing games with it at home: seating Mother at the table or opening and closing her car door, carrying her bags, getting Daddy's slippers, doing the dishes without being asked. You can put them up to doing something for the other parent or child. And they'll love it—especially some Sunday morning when *you* serve breakfast to *them* in bed!

There is genuine parent power in working and serving *with* your own kids. When at all times you are patient and consistent, courteous and kind, especially when you correct them, they will not only love you quite naturally, but they will respect you as their hero and heroine. That is what my father did for me.

14

Consistency and Unity

Almost in tears, a six-year-old boy spoke to me recently. Although he was not yet able to reason consistently, he heard about "all the people dying from cigarettes" and laid it before his mother, an average smoker. She hemmed and hawed and told him she couldn't quit.

"But my teacher could," he protested.

"I am not your teacher!" his mother answered loftily.

"But you told me that we should do what teacher does, and besides you said we should take care of our bodies." The little boy was adamant, and from the way he talked with me, I am certain that he was deeply concerned—as a knowing child should be.

"Bobby," she remonstrated impatiently, "can't you see that I am busy fixing supper? Now you sit down and practice your reading."

Bobby did. The book was on honesty. By the time he got to me, he had arrived at a logical conclusion: "I don't think my mom means what she says. I don't even think she cares much about me."

Parenting is a daily testing process. And this is good. It challenges you to be a better person, for you are under scrutiny. In a sense your children are testing you in one way or another every moment. If you tell them that a certain food is not good for them and then you eat it yourself, they will listen less carefully to your "wisdom" about what they should eat. If you tell them not to yell at each other but sometimes you yell at them, you just lost another round.

Our consistency tells just how honest we really are and how much we care, and our children's consistency will govern the direction they grow. Their consistency will be best learned and enforced by your tender, warm, consistent, and firm example. Here, above all places, self-control in *you* will nurture self-discipline in your young.

Consistency is such an all-pervasive essential for sound discipline that you will find it running like a strong thread throughout this book. Though brief, this may be the single most important chapter in this book; because of its total emphasis on consistency and our hope to avoid redundancy, we will not overdo it here. We include this chapter simply to insure clarity of our meanings and place the emphasis in appropriate context.

Assuming that you are a warm, loving person, consistency is the jewel of parenting that is your moment-by-moment goal. Happy and successful child rearing does not offer time for habitual scolding, slaps, and faultfinding interspersed with hugs and kisses. Children are as quick as fruit flies to find any spoilage in your system.

But don't be discouraged if you are not *perfectly* consistent. No one is. One of our dear friends who claims to have no religious urges, recently murmured, "Oh, God," when her two-year-old was testing her frustration level. I wonder if this was just an epithet or if even nonreligious folks don't unconsciously look to a higher power. You almost have to if you are to discover the jewel of consistency. Whether or not you believe that God helps those who help themselves, you will do well to keep in good physical condition—eating, drinking, resting, and exercising so that you can cope with both the family majors and minors, the stressful problems that so often tear many parents apart.

Set your goals carefully, plan your work, and work your plan. Do your best never to give a command and then forget it or fail to follow through; this is the sure road to defeat in family or school or any discipline anywhere. If you think it the better part of valor to change your order, let your children know, and if they are old enough, explain your reasons for making a change. Try to be honest in all things, and you will rest more easily.

Our son Dennis, who for many years had the benefit of Dorothy's and my trial-and-error methods, puts it this way: "Consistency of both your mood and your expectations shows a line of acceptable or unacceptable behavior. This provides stability for a child much as the fold provides security for a lamb. When your instructions and your manner say to your children, 'Thus far shall you go and no further,' you make it clear that they are set limits, not inconsistent, constantly shifting ones."

"You wouldn't have much respect for a parent who said, 'This is what you can get away with today, but tomorrow you won't know your limits until you get there. I may be in a bad mood and beat you up for the same thing I let you do today.' Yet, to a greater or lesser degree, this is the impression that our inconsistency often gives our children."

As one method toward your goal of consistency, Dennis suggests that you establish your "tentative tolerance threshold" (TTT) so that you clearly stop your children's negative activity before they push you over your TTT into an angry and inappropriate corrective action. Your TTT may be lower for some children than for others. Yet you will never *ever* allow your children to plague you into real anger, and will pray for grace to avoid harsh words and impatient acts.

This setting of a standard suggests to your children a consistency which makes them more secure so that they do not have to keep testing you constantly to see where your mood is at the moment. In turn, when they cease pushing on you, you feel better, more content and secure in your role. So we have a win-win situation instead of one in which all parties lose.

Here is an example of how it recently worked in one home:

135

Jan, the young mother realized all of a sudden that the noise of her four-year-old's toy nearby was getting on her nerves as she tried to concentrate on her letter writing. So she said gently, "Danny, Mommy wants you to stop playing with that noisy toy in the house. Please play with it outside."

But Danny pretended not to hear or may in fact have been concentrating so much that his young brain didn't get the full message. He may have thought that she just wanted him to be quieter.

So Jan sent her second, and last, instruction. This was her pre-set TTT. She had made her instructions clear and had decided on any given activity what she expects of each of her children in terms of developmental maturity, before she will deprive or punish, and well before she becomes frustrated and angry. This not only helps her children, but is a conscious reminder for self-control.

Jan has already set up her back-up system, her options for corrective action if one of her children does not respond. It may be deprivation of a cherished toy or a trip to the park or, depending on the age and circumstances, even a switching on the legs. But the punishment, if any, will be appropriate to the age. For example, you will not deprive a four-year-old of his tricycle for a month. That is *forever* for a child that age. But you may deprive him for the rest of the day or for today and tomorrow.

So Jan speaks again, gently but clearly, with her eyes directly on his and with a sense of finality: "Danny, Mother asked you to take that toy out of the house if you want to play with it. Would you like to have me take it away for the rest of the day?"

"No," the little boy answers and takes the toy out of the house.

If he had not obeyed, Jan's options were all set.

Your TTT should be established in counsel with your spouse so that there is unity in consistency. Otherwise there will be confusion. And your TTT plan will be made at some quiet time when there is no ominous disciplinary situation threatening.

Whether you use TTT or not, develop your own plan for consistency, and then work your plan. When your children perceive that you are unselfish, firm, and honest, your road to the fine art of discipleship will be a much more creative and delightful one.

15

Learning How to Think

No wonder Thomas Edison's mother was so angry at Tom's teachers who declared him to be stupid and ill-behaved. Young Tom found little or no challenge in the rigid boundaries of classroom instruction. His creativity stifled, his fantasies grounded, he begged out of the mental prison. His fine mind clearly was not being challenged, and he rebelled against the stupor being imposed upon him by a stolid pedagogue. He refused the extrusion process in which most students come out the same-sized bologna and went home to have fun in real-life learning by observing, experimenting, and creating.

Exactly the same havoc is being wrought on our children before our very faces these days as we blithely look on. All indications are that something is wrong with "the system," but we are so much prisoners of convention that we can't believe the ball is in our court. Besides it is inconvenient to be bothered, so we turn the other way. Then we wonder why we reap such horrendous failure and delinquency in an era when our children should be riding high in all areas. In fact, we are finding that warm, responsive parents who educate their children at home usually bring out genius in some area, such as art, music, electronics, writing, astronomy, and other sciences.

Think for a moment of your own children. If you are normal parents and have normal children, you have often thought and sometimes voiced how bright they are. Yet you somehow do not equate them with those geniuses of the ages simply because you consider yourselves "ordinary people." Mrs. Edison did not give in to that temptation. She saw something in her son that others did not see. And you can do the same, likely with genius results. If you do not do what she did, your children will likely fulfill your expectations of ordinariness.

Learning to be thinkers rather than mere reflectors of others' thoughts should be a constant goal in the education of your children, both for their academic achievement and for character's sake. If you help your children to think through the consequences of their thoughts and actions and to realize that one day they inevitably must face those consequences in one way or another, they are more likely to be on their way to sound behavior.

The recipe for making thinkers is simple, but requires your close, affectionate, and consistent attention to your children:

First, your truthful responsiveness (and again we stress consistency) is crucial. Don't give them a silly answer one time and a serious one another. This does not mean you have no humor, for the best of humor is not farcical, but grows out of real life incidents. Joking and jesting, on the other hand, are being humorous just for the sake of being funny, and are never appropriate if you want stable thinkers.

Second, remember not to expect much deep or consistent thoughtfulness of children under age eight, and even less if they are younger.

Third, beginning at around ages three to five, ask *why* and *how* questions, first very simple ones and then more complex as they grow older. Don't demand deep or complex answers until the age range of about eight to twelve (but be happy and especially attentive if your child has achieved this cognitive readiness earlier). Yet don't feel disappointed if your child is a slow developer; he may be the brightest of all.

Around ages three to five, you can ask or answer such questions as "Why does Daddy leave every morning?" (He goes to work). Or "How do you get water out of the faucet?" (Turn it on). Or yet, "Why does ice float?" (It has air inside, making it lighter than water). Eventually you may have to answer questions like "Why do you and Daddy always sleep together?" Or "Why do older people snore?" Or yet "How do you make babies, Mama?"

There is always a risk involved, of course, when children are encouraged to think. A key challenge will be how *attentive* and responsive you can be to their questions and the consistency of your sound example. Otherwise they will look to others.

This was a principal cause for the famed student rebellions of the sixties. The leaders were thinking people, many of whom were sound in their thinking but wrong in their methods; many others, however, were unsound in both thought and method. The followers, however brilliant and able, were peer dependent youths who had never learned to think for themselves or to get the total picture on anything. Some of their ideas were sound enough but without balance or care on how best to implement them. Others of their concoctions were devastating for the nation.

Many of them were highly idealistic and developed important reforms in diet and in service to others. Yet at the same time they couched their reforms in a setting of indulgent, irresponsible, and perverted behavior, which bred filth, disease, and often crime. University professors, media entrepreneurs, and others were vocal while parents and pastors looked on with little apparent interest or effort.

In the first place, we start our children out wrong when we force them into any institutional care before they are able to reason consistently. No teacher or caretaker can listen, respond, and provide the love and firmness that are needed in these early years. Formal academic pressures, whether at home or school, may force a child to learn many facts but will fail to allow the child to attain his or her maximum cognitive development. Such reasoning skills as putting oneself in another's place, abstract thinking, and moral judgments of right and wrong cannot be taught to children on a consistent basis until they are around eight to twelve years old—the ages when, as we have written elsewhere in this book, they reach cognitive readiness.

Many schools, realizing that their children are not ready for such thoughtful studies, simply give them workbookish nonsense, which is boring and stifles their imaginations, which are normally so excited in their early years. We give them adult-contrived fantasies such as *Sesame Street* and *Mickey Mouse*. We then proceed to institutionalize and conventionalize this foolishness in the classroom almost to the point of reverence, when in fact it deprives our youngsters of doing their own thing.

Because of time constraints and other pressures, teachers tend to handle classes by having students memorize facts for tests rather than helping them apply principles, digest, assimilate, and organize information. Such technique makes the student more or less dependent on the judgment and perception of others.

Look again at the findings of Professor McCurdy when he was preparing the report on genius for the Smithsonian Institution: Your children need (1) a great deal of *you*, (2) very little of their agemates, and (3) a rich experience in exploring for themselves.[1] Somehow young Tom Edison's mother understood this. It mattered not for her that she did not have a college education, nor will it for you.

What does matter is that you give your children a lot of warm responsiveness. *Do not rush them into formal study* at home or in school, but in due time see that they have the basic learning skills of the Western world, and open the doors—in libraries, at home, in the great outdoors—for them to search for themselves. Otherwise they will fail to reach their potential because they have been sent to school before they were cognitively ready for what they would experience.

As was implied earlier, children who are taught to think for themselves invariably will be asking more *whys* and *hows* and few *whats, wheres,* and *whens,* which are the questions answered by the curriculum in most conventional schools today. And when we give them the right models they get more than the instructional picture; they gain an experience. Their instruction becomes three dimensional. When we do, we will have many more George Washingtons and George Washington Carvers; Benjamin Franklins and Andrew Carnegies; Abraham Lincolns and Wright brothers; Abigail Adams's, Pearl Bucks and Sandra Day O'Connors. Already we are seeing a great many such youngsters in the home school renaissance, which harks back to the educational practices that gave us such men and women through the history of America.

When you are warm and responsive, a consistent comrade to your children, you will build a creative integrity. As they grow into ages of consistent reasonability, they will think things through in a sound way and will be safe for the family democracy. Such children are much better candidates for self-control, the kind of discipline which will be a credit to you. They have that quality of self-worth which is altogether more productive than mere self-esteem. They will be creative, free-enterprising individuals of the kind who build strong families and great nations.

Encouragement and Appreciation

E ncouragement is a much sharper discipline tool than is punishment, although the latter may sometimes be necessary, on occasion even a switch or a strap. Hands-on warmth builds understanding between parents and children when you reward for obedience, not indulgence. There is great disciplinary sense in the bumper sticker that asks, "Have you hugged your child today?"

Such gestures endow your children with a sense of your confidence, pride, security, and love. An occasional hug or touch provides that valued third dimension. If you are consistent and warm in your displays of gratitude and affection, they will understand when you have to restrict or punish them.

Loving affection is a precious expression of the Golden Rule, which should be natural to most parents, yet many find it hard to carry out. Some among us were reared by families in which the loving hug or pat or appropriate caress was seldom if ever known. If you are one of these, don't be reluctant to learn from others. Place yourself in the company of families to whom the expression of affection and gratitude is second nature, and take your children with you. Speaking and showing affection without "feeling" warm and loving will help create the feeling, and it will become easier to express love. Be patient, for such changes of nature do not come easily. Simply remember that every normal person appreciates warm acknowledgment.

Bear in mind that each of your children is different. These differences are not their fault nor yours, except as your example may have led them or as your habits may have influenced them during pregnancy as for example, by smoking or by using drugs, alcohol, or too much tea or coffee. Your goal will be to never try to make them alike except in those character and personality qualities that all good people should have, such as love, kindness, patience, compassion, integrity, dependability, and order. You will try to maximize their strengths and minimize their weaknesses.

Of two brothers who visited us the other day, the younger is naturally outgoing, unselfish, interested in everyone and everything, but he is short on memory and not very orderly. The older boy is inclined to be introverted, defensive, and interested in others for his own sake, but he is orderly, dependable, and has a memory like the proverbial elephant. Their mother is well aware of their individual differences. Her goal is to give each of them a sense of responsibility and a concern for each other and for those less fortunate than they.

She takes care never to make the virtues of the younger a burden to the older, but does remind the older of his example to the younger—which adds to the sense of worth which he more urgently needs. We have taken great pleasure in watching their progress under her careful direction. The younger boy is making remarkable progress in orderliness, and his big brother is teaching him to tie a bow knot—a thoughtfulness and skill *which their mother duly notes,* and which is almost automatic in building self-worth in the older boy as well as respect from his little brother. At the same time this service to his brother is helping to wipe out his natural selfishness.

If your thoughtfulness is expressed consistently, you will rapidly build a base for sound discipline, which as we have noted elsewhere is discipleship at its best. If you neglect complimenting your children for their behavior and good works, if you show affection only when you want a favor, if you are erratic in your kindness and encouragement, expect an erratic child. Your children whom you do not deliberately enjoy in their early years will not enjoy you in later years. Gratitude expressed with affection is the oil that lubricates a fine disciplinary machine.

Appreciation is in short supply these days. Try a little research of your own: have each family member who is old enough to do it keep a record of each word or act (hug, gift, etc.) of appreciation for one day. Later on, extend your study to several days or one day weekly for a month. The results will be revealing and will usually stimulate more expressions of love and gratitude. The damaging effect of one negative comment on a child's image can be so great that it takes four or five hugs or rewards to undo one negative word or action.

Dorothy tells how her mother "conned" her into enjoying work. She would tell little "Doto" how well she cleaned and dusted because her "little fingers could get into the corners better than mother's big fingers." Or she would tell her how happy she was when a drawer or cupboard was cleaned and straightened. Dorothy used to do drawers, closets, and cupboards for her mother until her death, at age ninety-six, the last seven years of which were in our home.

Science has come at least partly to the rescue in explaining what happens when one person through genuine encouragement and gratitude brings out radiantly positive responses in another. We call it the "endorphin response" or ER. Endorphins are positive hormone "elves" secreted by adrenaline into the body systems when your experiences with others are upbeat. They promote the precise opposite to the negative, depressed feeling which you have when someone does you a bad turn or ignores you. Dorothy's mom was a past master at generating endorphins, and you can be, too.

For example, you can ask your boy, "Bobby, do you think you'll be able to clean your room by yourself today?" Or you can growl, "Bobby, can't you ever clean your room by yourself?" The first invites and reinforces success. The second turns back success feelings even if Bobby completes the job; it is a harbinger of total defeat.

We watched an older sister use the same psychology on her younger sister who had asked to play with big sis's doll. "I know you'll be extra careful with my dolls today," the older sister said as she gave the doll to her younger sister. The little girl beamed—from encouragement and appreciation!

Health: Diet, Dress, Sleep, and Exercise

The other day while flying from Chicago to Portland, Oregon, we noticed a young mother and her young children across the aisle in the airplane. When refreshments were served, she gave her baby a few sips of champagne and her five-year-old his own glass of cola drink. When she raised her eyes as if desiring our approval, she showed that she knew better but seemed to think that champagne was cute since it was her little daughter's birthday.

Yet many parents don't even know better. They don't bother to equate the potential of their actions with the effect on their children or try to think of a more constructive way to celebrate. Far too many ignorant or indifferent mothers and dads freely hand over soft drinks and sugared or fatty foods at their children's every beck and call.[1] We see this on virtually every plane flight we take across the nation and at many restaurants and in countless homes that we visit. If it is not the parents, it is an uninformed flight attendant or waitress who urges such expediencies on you and your young and who does not have the wisdom to give the child something better from which to choose.

Nor are these people the ignorant poor. Many, if not most, are from homes of those who should know better—physicians, nurses, teachers, pastors, contractors, attorneys, mechanics, and businessmen. We have found dentists generally to be the most careful of all, yet we have been surprised to find that even many of them are not aware of the hidden dangers in nearly all processed foods and of the way that snacking—sugar or no sugar—cruelly insults the bodies and teeth of our children.

In chapter 4 we asked how you would treat a fine car. How would you expect it to behave if you gave it leaded gasoline when the factory specified unleaded? Or if you used diesel oil instead of gasoline, or vice versa? Would you run it on tires that are underinflated? Would you never mind about anti-freeze in below-zero weather? Would you slam it into reverse when you are rolling down a hill? Would you look for repairs at the local blacksmith shop?

Yet many of us use less sense about how we feed our children, clothe them, and rush them into activities that will tear out their "transmissions." Then we wonder why they don't behave, are impatient, fail in school, or rebel at home. Even worse, we commonly fail to realize that we can't replace parts on our children as we can on cars, especially in their guiding mechanisms, their brains.

This lack of information or commonsense in practice directly obstructs sound discipline. You are fortunate if you can find a physician competent in nutritional sciences. This may be partially explained by a National Research Council study of the nation's medical schools, which revealed that over half of these institutions offer fewer than half the classroom hours in nutrition recommended by the Council. The national medical board examinations, which all students must pass to obtain a license, ignore whole areas of nutrition.[2]

If modern medicine has made anything clear, it is the certainty that your *life-style* will predict your behavior and health. Many families are practicing *death styles*. Yet there are few areas, if any, where parents are more touchy or more expedient or indulgent of themselves or their children. What, when, and how much you eat will make a lot of difference in the way you react to your family or classroom. Genuine reform is rare. Yet, unfortunately, diet is a sacred cow with most of us. And our own and our children's dress is largely dictated by our peers. Status and pride can place us in compromising situations which dilute our effectiveness and example as disciplinarians. The use of our leisure time is nobody's business. Yet the way we manage these, along with sleep and exercise, will largely dictate how much will be exacted from our health and behavior or how much we will show the patience and wisdom so important to leadership in discipline.

Some of the information we provide you here may be so new and strange to you that it appears to be exaggerated or the idle dream of another health theorist. Yet every illustration is actual and all scientific claims have been carefully checked.

Diet

What you and your children eat bears directly on the nature and number of discipline problems you will have around your home. It is impossible to have completely self-directed, self-controlled children with sound physical and emotional health if you allow them to eat what and when their natural appetites dictate. Although we provide much more detail and documentation in our new book on family health, we feel compelled to lay down a few principles and methods here as absolute conditions for well-behaved children.

Among the most common devils that torment your children, induce crankiness, and make discipline unpleasant are sugar and snacks. While we do not offer cure-alls, nearly all acutely hyperactive or delinquent children who are brought to us have a rather heavy diet of sugar, refined grains, and fatty foods.

White sugar, white rice, white bread, corn chips and potato chips, cookies, doughnuts and cake, and sweetened breakfast cereals, often with milk, are common garbage for our struggling children today. Some feel that milk combines with sugar to ferment in their stomachs and even, to a limited extent, to intoxicate. Large amounts and varieties of most foods at a given meal also tend to slow brain activity, as the blood is drawn away from the brain and into the stomach area to accommodate digestion.

Jan, a Southwestern mother, called Dorothy one day, distraught about the embarrassment her children (a girl and boy ages seven and five respectively) were causing because they were getting really fussy about what they would eat. Their outbursts occurred most often at dinnertime, because their breakfast was pretty much "cut and dried" and there was little they could do about the menus at school—which they supplemented from the fast-food machines, financed by their allowances.

But now the "thing" was getting out of control: they were refusing or complaining about the food set before them when guests were present and even when they and their parents were guests at the tables of friends. It was becoming very trying to both parents to have to contend with their fussing, and coaxing and bribing with dessert often ended in unpleasantness.

"I am at my wit's end," Jan cried out to Dorothy and in the same breath admitted that she had given her children "almost everything they have ever wanted."

"But," interrupted Dorothy, "have you given them what they *needed?*"

"What do you mean?"

"I mean that children find their greatest security in having to 'push up against' someone who is stronger than they. If you do not show that strength and show it in a consistent way, they will flail out in any way they can until they find someone who is willing to be their strong model."

Dorothy could have given Jan the advice commonly found in newspaper columns: to tenderly try to lead them into some compromise. But she didn't. After questioning Jan a little further, Dorothy counseled her to *start now, this evening.*

"Have your plan well in hand," Dorothy advised. "Be sure your husband is with you in this. Set before them at least one very small serving—perhaps no more—that they normally turn down. Be sure that you are well rested. Pray for patience. And then say *very calmly* something like this, 'I'm sorry, but that's what we're having for dinner. If you don't want to eat it, you may get down from the table, but otherwise you are to eat it without fussing. Then you may have some other things.'"

Dorothy also advised Jan to direct her remarks to Cindy, the older and obviously more influential of the two. Together they planned how Don, Jan's husband, would quietly support her by saying, "That's it. Mother's absolutely right and those are the rules."

The next day over the phone Jan almost shouted to Dorothy and me, "It worked! It's a whole new day! Cindy didn't even question me from the start, and Jimmy looked over at her in surprise and did exactly as she did. What an example of *example!*"

"And of firmness and consistency . . . and love!" Dorothy added.

"This does not mean that you will be totally rigid," Dorothy admonished, "for children probably do have the right to like some things better than others and even perhaps one or two dislikes, but be very careful about this, because they can multiply and get out of control. The best consistent rule is that everybody eats some of everything before he has more of his favorite things. The example of parents and older children is vital here."

Tastes and eating habits are developed, not inherited, though family patterns are significant because of the strong influence of parental attitudes and example, which affect children's habits. Wise introduction of foods to the infant and firm but loving management of the young child will help your child to enjoy a variety of healthful foods. As we mentioned earlier, your reason and example must reign at least until your children reach the age of consistent reasonability—which psychologists call "cognitive readiness." That sometimes does not

151

come until they are ten or twelve years old, and it seems to make little difference whether they are average or very bright.

Even then your nutritional rules should be followed as long as your children are at your table. This is different from peer dependency; it is parental principle and example. This, in old-fashioned terms, is called *good manners.* You must insist that they learn such courtesies for their own good if they are ever to amount to anything in a world where responsibility must be insured before authority can be granted and where they must learn to get along with others if they want others to get along with them. *You* are the first person with whom they should learn to get along.

Dress-Power

There is no more *accurate* predictor of children's behavior than their dress. Nor are there many factors which more powerfully affect their health. *This Week Magazine* published a case in point some years ago: the Buffalo, New York, high school's "Magic Mirror." Students were increasingly unhappy with general student conduct on campus, and one day they discussed this with their English teacher. Or perhaps *she* wisely induced their question. The student consensus suggested that if the students would be more modest, tasteful, and mannerly in their dress, it might make a difference in their behavior.

With their teacher's and principal's permission and the co-operation of the student body, they installed large mirrors at the head of each stairway where they could face themselves often throughout the day. Soon boys began to wear trousers that were not quite so close-fitting and began to comb their hair neatly. Before long, pressed trousers, polished shoes, shirts, ties, and sweaters or jackets became the peer standard. Girls fixed their hair in attractive but practical ways and turned more to skirts than tight shorts and jeans. They no longer wore T-shirts without bras, and it was standard to wear blouses underneath their sweaters and jackets. The accompanying improved behavior was so obvious that it became the talk of the town. The psychology of cleanliness, order, and self-respect worked even beyond the hopes of the students and their teachers.

Modesty is a powerful aid in developing sound family discipline and long-term self-control, both in the family and in the community. For example, very short skirts or very tight trousers on adolescents invite lust. Prudish? If that is what you want to call it, but anyone who has worked with youth and adults knows that risqué dress does not encourage good behavior.

A large swimming pool came with our home when it was donated to the Hewitt Research Foundation. We share it widely with our community since it is the only pool around, and we have witnessed many examples of poolside dress and the reactions it brings, particularly with the extremely brief and tight swimsuits and bikinis, which hardly disguise that which they are meant to cover. Whenever bikinis abound, young males seem to move in like bees to blossoms at honey time. This behavior has induced us old-fashioned prudes to require parental chaperonage at all mixed parties.

The Therapy of Dress

I learned the value and the appropriateness of covering the limbs in another way in 1953 from Dr. Erwin Syphers, then the head physician at a leading American hospital in Tokyo. He found that I was developing bronchiectasis, a permanent inflammation of the bronchial tubes, particularly dangerous in Japan, where tuberculosis was rampant during those post-World War II years. He gave me no medicines, but sent me home to do two things: to drink at least two quarts of water a day—other than at meal time—in order to cleanse my system and to keep my arms and legs "just as well clothed" as my body.

153

It seems that the heart and lungs rely very heavily on the extremities, especially the legs, for their pumping motion and for oxygenating the blood. If the limbs are allowed to get cold, the blood vessels become constricted and slow the flow of the blood. The result is less oxygen to the blood and thence to the body.

The inappropriately dressed child as well as adult is in trouble and often on the road to illness. Shoes that are too tight, inadequately clothed limbs, clothes that are too tight at the waist where they restrict the breathing and free movement of the abdominal organs, and uncovered heads in cold weather are other areas which can cause harm to your children's health. Unhealthy children are unhappy people, and unhappy youngsters are more difficult to control.

Sleep: Resting for Control

If you want a relaxed and cooperative and better disciplined tribe in your home, try giving them more efficient sleep. Some parents and children get too much sleep. They are often indolent, lethargic, tending to lie around instead of being constructively active. Many do not get enough sleep. But we believe that relatively few utilize sleep as they should, and the result is impatience, impetuousness, neurosis, and oftentimes physical and mental breakdown.

If you want to double your working time so as to have more time for yourself and to avoid the constant cry of your children and spouse, "I don't have time!" try several of these ideas on sleep:

First, those who have a heavy daily load of work and study and who would like to enjoy some quiet time without the temptations of television and the phone need to utilize the early morning hours. When these people make up their minds to try rising early, they often forget that they are "night persons" and become early birds. One medical school experiment found that student efficiency ranged from three to five times as great in the hours before breakfast as those after supper.

Second, world authorities suggest that the most productive time to sleep is between late afternoon and the few hours after midnight. They add that the hours before midnight provide two or three times as much effective rest for the body as the hours between midnight and sunlight. This means that a person going to sleep at 8:00 or 9:00 P.M. can awake fully restored by three or four in the morning. We do not insist that these early hours are vital for all families, but early retiring and early rising set the stage for a far more efficient day. This is especially true for mothers and fathers who need extra time for quiet study or meditation.

Third, eat early and lightly before bedtime, if at all. Try drinking a glass of cool water when your appetite is sharp but you know it is better not to eat. Go for a walk or take other mild exercise if you do eat. Have a tepid shower. It will relax you. Keep your mind on quiet themes. Many reserve bedtime for meditation and worship. Go to bed early, if possible at the same time as your young children, and you have the experts' best recipe for satisfying sleep that builds self-controlled families.

If you still have a hard time getting to sleep or returning to sleep once you have wakened, try breathing deeply. Take even five to ten additional breaths without exhaling and soon you will be yawning. Keep this up, along with meditation and *positive,* serene thoughts, and sleep is more likely to overtake you.

Patient, wise adult example is almost impossible without a rested body. Likewise, it is unreasonable for you to make severe demands on a tired, inexperienced child. Sleep combined with a light supper, a brief, tepid shower or bath, and light exercise puts together a proven recipe. We stress light suppers, preferably of fresh fruits and grains such as whole-

155

grained zwieback for supper, because the stomach-emptying time is reduced from four to six hours down to about two hours. Your stomach should be empty when you go to bed. A quiet, resting stomach is important to a dreamless or peaceful sleep, and heavy suppers just before bedtime often bring troubled sleep, sometimes even contributing to nightmares.

The Discipline of Exercise

While there are references to exercise in our chapters on child development, we dare not overlook it as essential to basic living and self-control, including its adaptability to family life. Take your choice between gardening, running, biking, cross-country skiing, swimming, participating in sports, or just plain walking. Make sure you do, but don't overdo. The right kind of exercise builds your muscles, heart, circulation, and respiration at the same time that it also tones or relaxes you and helps your attitude and temperament.

Gardening is generally considered a valued or necessary exercise for most people in most countries except in the United States. We have watched—and helped—as our friends in Japan bent over to cultivate, plant, weed, and harvest. Simple home gardening is a complete exercise if fully and appropriately used.

As we have traveled by train through Europe, we have noticed fertile, well-ordered fruit and/or vegetable gardens in the back yards of nearly all homes. Even small city gardens a few feet square can be highly productive. Dorothy has enjoyed some even on her window sills and kitchen decks.

When your children learn lessons of orderly rows; of careful mulching, weeding, cultivating; and of the seed giving itself that others might live, a creative discipline comes into play that is often exciting to a youngster's imagination. The young mind, together with active, skillful hands, makes exercise more enjoyable—especially when done with *you*.

We do not condemn running, either for children or adults,

but it is becoming increasingly apparent that many are suffering knee, foot, or internal injuries from the constant and unnatural pounding that many runners subject themselves to. This is especially true of those who do not have the right equipment or do not know how to run. There are other forms of exercise which are more often recommended for the average person, particularly those who have physical problems and women who want to avoid all risk of internal harm.

Biking has become increasingly popular and does not involve the physical risks of running: damage to feet, legs, abdominal organs, and even the heart. Yet bikers are cautioned to cycle in safe places and to abide by traffic laws. Here again, attention should be given, if possible, to obtaining safe equipment and keeping it adjusted and in good running order—well-oiled, seat height adjusted, and brakes in good repair.

Swimming is an excellent experience for those who do not have an aversion to water and who understand its dangers. It is often healing because of its warmth or cold. Tennis also lends itself well to playing without undue rivalry. Courts are widely available free at parks and schools. And golf, although usually more expensive than tennis, can be enjoyed as competition with par more than with people. When I used to play golf, I found, like many others, that trying to lower my score as near as possible to par (golf experts' standard score for any given golf course) improved my game far more than to bet a quarter with companion golfers on each hole.

When we were living in Michigan, Dorothy and I often enjoyed cross-country skiing together or with our family or neighbors. It is quiet, beautiful, and may be the best exercise of all, with the possible exception of walking—which is more nearly universal.

Managing Money

The Sullivan Sisters Sitting Service near Orlando, Florida, is an example of an effective family industry run by children which began with neighbors' requests for competent babysitting. These girls not only do babysitting, but also have become deeply involved in candy-striping at the nearby Florida Hospital—much as any sound business sees related enterprises and reaches out to meet the need. But not one of these girls receives money from Mom and Dad. They don't need to. Three of them average about $35 weekly, using their money for their own clothes, savings, and church.

Money can be one of the most onerous problems in family discipline. Young people's wants usually far exceed their needs, and if wants are permitted to carry the day, you are in trouble. There is enough trouble between spouses without asking for more from your children. Take a careful look at the way you mix money and kids if you want any peace. We cannot recall witnessing behavior problems in a single family in which parents were firm and consistent in seeing that their children basically worked their own ways.

If you give any amount of your time to magazine or newspaper or radio or television news, you have heard over and over again how credit cards are defiling the American economy. Yet it is not the card that is in error, but the self-control, the self-discipline of the users. The same principle applies to children who assume that parents will dish out an unending helping of credit, whether or not the children work for it or obligate themselves to repay.

Establish this idea well in your own head: your children do not have any right to the money which *you* earn. Other than real *needs* they may have in terms of future schooling and security, you can also find better places to leave your money when you die. The principle here is to build self-dependence, independence of *you*.

They only have right to money they earn and that only under your own guidance as long as you think wise. For example, your boy or girl may have a newspaper route or magazine subscription business or muffin and sandwich business, to name a few current projects. Whether or not the money is theirs or part of the family treasury must be determined by you or with them in family council, depending on their ages and maturity. Some families in poverty depend in part upon the earnings of their children.

Allowances are common to Western families, but that does not make them desirable. Sometimes they may work, but they often appeal to selfish motives and keep children tied to their parents when they should be building independence. If you do decide to pay them, instead of encouraging an outside job such as a paper route, we suggest that you pay only for work that is for the general good of the family and not for work that is their duty. Why pay children for making their own beds and cleaning their own rooms? Who else is sleeping there? Why pay for doing the dishes? Mother and Father share in the procurement and preparation of the food, so why shouldn't the children share in the kitchen too, even if just for the sake of learning the skills available there?

In your children's early years, decide what things they should do for themselves. Work this out with them later on, as they grow older and can grasp the meanings of authority and responsibility. Some parents designate certain jobs, which are not unique to the children's needs and wants, and pay for them: washing Dad's pickup truck. Or cleaning the windows on the house. Or learning and doing minor repairs. Or weeding the garden. Don't make money too easy to get. They need to work for it.

It is not appropriate in this book to outline principles of money management, investments, and other aspects of the economy. You will find many discussions on family industries; one of them is our book *Home Style Teaching* and in other books in your local library or available through interlibrary loan. Our principle concern here is that you begin to teach your children an appreciation, but not greed, for money at an early age.

Among the best methods to build altruism into your children is to teach them to give of themselves and their resources to others. Many church-going families teach their children from age one or two to drop their coins into the offering basket. Some teach the biblical ideal of tithing. Others educate their young to respond to various charities, beginning with those primarily concerned with children. As we point out repeatedly in this book, there are few therapies so effective in building outgoing and self-disciplined children as manual work and service—of giving themselves like the seed that goes into the ground that their lives might be multiplied for others.

So money—or barter—can be one of your best disciplinary tools. But it is important that you use it rightly. Children must learn how to use it for others, and not to worship it as an end for themselves.

PART FOUR

THE MINISTRY OF TENDERNESS

The Parent or Teacher Putdown

K elly tells the story of her mother's response to her desire
to take typing in high school. It was an extra half-unit per
semester and took a full extra hour at school. She promised
her mother that she would get all her chores done and would
even do them better than ever if she could only take typing.

"But you just don't have it in you, Kelly," her mother declared. "You know you are all thumbs."

"But . . ." Kelly began to tell of her ambitions. And she knew
her shortcomings: she wanted to practice changing from all
thumbs to skilled fingers.

"But nothing," her mother reacted thoughtlessly. "You just
do not have the talents along those mechanical lines."

Kelly traces her fears of dealing with anything mechanical to
this day, thirty years later, to that exchange. But she secretly
began learning to type and now sails easily along at ninety to
one hundred words a minute. Her fine skill is crucial to her
employment.

We wing our way blithely along with our children, convinced that the greatest cruelty they know is on the playground, in the classroom, or on the bus. And indeed these
can be among the worst. We bemoan the horrors of child
abuse as an act of the pervert, the mentally ill parent, the alcoholic parent, or the parent who is under great pressure from
financial or other stress. We hardly consider the effects of un-
thinking words or acts around the house, of ignoring our children and damaging them, which can lead to fear, uncertainty

and sorrow, and the sense of rejection—one of the worst abuses of all.

Without intending to demean their children, parents often leave them with scars that linger a lifetime and sometimes evoke despair. This is one of the most certain and easiest ways to create your own discipline problems. Some of this comes from parental ego; some is simply thoughtlessness of the tender feelings of your young. Sometimes we say demeaning things about our children to others. Sometimes we say them to our children themselves. On occasion such words are picked up by other children in the family, and they torment the child with the same abuse.

Negative Remarks

Such putdowns come in many forms—ridiculing, faultfinding, unfavorably comparing, allowing no court of appeal, negative name-calling, giving the silent treatment, and more. Some of these will not be yours. Yet there are few of us who do not have a part in some kind of putdown during the day, either as parent, spouse, teacher, or child. In order to build family loyalty, putdowns between siblings as well as physical attacks should be forbidden, and you must set the example, not only with your children but with your own sibling relationships—their aunts and uncles.

Kim's experience was quite different from Kelly's. Her mother was proud of her many abilities and even bragged beyond them. But one day she came home from school using a naughty word, which shocked her puritanical mother and the meaning of which Kim did not fully understand.

"Where on earth did you learn that?" her mother demanded.

"We-e-ell," Kim began to answer.

"At school," her mother insisted without waiting for an answer. "That church school is a corrupt place."

"But I didn't learn it at school," declared Kim. Yet she could not, to her mother's satisfaction, tell how she picked up the nasty word.

When Kim's mother took her to enroll in the second grade the next September, she told the new teacher that Kim was really a good girl but had some trouble with telling the truth. With Kim standing there, she cited her daughter's problem with the naughty word. The teacher quickly dismissed the little girl from the conversation, but the terror of that experience on her sensitive spirit has never left her.

That year when there was any disruption in the classroom and the teacher asked the children, "Who did it?" she almost always kept Kim in for recess to try to pry the name of the culprit out of her even though the little girl insisted she did not know. In a variation of this distrust, the teacher one day asked her students to write out one of the ten commandments. Kim chose the fourth, the longest of all, and wrote it perfectly. The next day the teacher asked her to stand up and give it orally. But Kim, a shy creature at her boldest, froze and couldn't speak a word. Without any further check on her knowledge, such as another chance to write it out, the teacher accused her of cheating.

Already made insecure by her mother's putdown, Kim was devastated by her teacher's unfair and erratic assessments and by her own unsuccessful recital of one of the ten commandments. The teacher did not even have the commonsense or thoughtfulness to realize that the child would hardly cheat when the long fourth commandment was so important to her that she wrote it rather than the four-word commandment "Thou shalt not kill" or "Thou shalt not steal"—which was precisely what most of the children did.

Kim made up her mind that one day she was going to be a teacher who expected the best from her children and gave them her fullest confidence. Today she is one of America's leading people in her teaching field.

Dave had a father who was strong in almost every way,

sometimes too strong. His father did not particularly value a college education and told Dave that if he wanted one, he could get it himself. Dave took him at his word and at age nineteen left home, hitch-hiking north most of the length of California to his favorite college where he would work his way and also receive the best training in his chosen field.

Dave also left behind his girl friend, Sally, who attended a Southern California school, since her parents wanted her closer to home. Deeply in love, Dave and Sally agreed to correspond and meet each other at vacation times. But Dave's father was piqued at his leaving, perhaps ego-damaged, and one day dropped a word to Sally's mother that Dave "might not amount to much." The result was firm parental counsel to Sally to drop Dave, which she eventually did, with considerable grief for both.

Dave was for years mystified and depressed at his loss, for he knew that his and Sally's relationship ran deep. She was neither fickle nor unstable. Years later, after Dave had become a national figure, Sally's mother, now proud of her daughter's former boy friend, dropped word of the conversation with Dave's dad—almost as a joke. But it didn't endear his dad to him.

We stress here the possibility of innocence—or thoughtlessness—on the parts of all involved. Neither parent was deliberately trying to hurt Dave, yet both leveled heavy blows at his self-worth. Parental thoughtfulness as well as consistency is crucial if we are to build a desirable self-confidence in our children.

My eighth-grade teacher was possibly the best I ever had at any level. Yet, loving and wise as she was, she was also naive. One day as we were lining up to return to class after lunch, one of the boys used a word which had a double meaning— especially for boys. As the youngest and least mature, I snickered. Teacher took me aside to question me, but I could not possibly reveal the nasty connotation of that word. She would never have understood. So I was treated as defiant and was disciplined—to the delight of the boys involved and the chagrin of the rest of the students, who knew I had said or done nothing wrong.

Nancy Clark tells how a quite incidental remark caused Matilda Kipfer to "really hate" herself and to "live out" her hurts for much of her life. She was the youngest of fourteen children in a poverty-ridden home when an older brother observed, "Mom and Dad have too many children." Thoughtless, immature, no harm intended, he did the kind of damage which is sometimes never undone. Today, profiting by her hurts, Mrs. Kipfer is widely known as a counselor who helps women in New York State overcome the putdowns in their lives.

I remember well the time someone told me how my Aunt Minnie remarked that I would be a hopelessly retarded hydrocephalic. As the only nurse in the family, her word was heard as authority by the relatives. Fortunately for me, except for the physical pain it caused at birth, my dear mother did not worry that my head was so large. It is still large, yet I can wear a conventional size 7-1/2 hat. But even that momentary doubt worried me for years as a child. A more serious danger than having a large head, I learned later, was to have "the big head."

These are all true stories with fortunate endings. Yet many or most do not turn out this way. Carelessness with words—or no words—is a no-no wherever we go. Yet being unthoughtful of others in the family offers the greatest danger of all. If you fail to look at matters through others' eyes or "walk in their shoes" and anticipate their needs, you can make sound discipline all but impossible. The Golden Rule should reign here. When we determine to do to others as we would like to have them do to us, we will bring our tongues under close control.

Early Institutionalization

One of the most pervasively practiced putdowns of all is the institutionalizing of our children before they are ready. You will hear justification once in a while about the importance of getting children into the classroom early. These are either statements of ignorance, or they are lies. There is no series of replicated, or replicable, studies in the world which points in this direction. History records that every time a society has gone this route, the family and society have collapsed.

We are well aware of these claims for preschools and probably can quote more of them than most researchers and scholars, for we analyzed more than eight thousand studies in a project we did for the Office of Economic Opportunity and the U.S. Community Services Administration.[1] What in fact we are doing when we school our children before ages eight to twelve is inviting anxiety, frustration, failure, peer dependency, delinquency, and a low quality of socialization. In other words, we are a threat to our children, performing them a disservice, often ending in tragedy, seldom in ability and genius.

Effect on Ability

Many schools do a superior job, and others survive under severe trials created largely by indifferent parents. Yet America's decline in literacy during the public school growth years clearly proves McCurdy and the *Smithsonian* right.[2] Warm responsive parents and good homes are essential to improved schools. If children do not have enough time in their home nests to learn self-control, they have a much harder time in institutional life, where the rule is peer control.

Traditional schools obviously have a significant place in our society, and we can do many things which are not now being done to improve them. But it is no excuse to demean the home and to damage our children only because men are so preoccupied with their work and recreation and women so set on their "freedoms" that children are conveniently institutionalized. Parents must be ultimately held more responsible than schools, lest our free society collapse.

The rushing of little children early into school, often on the erroneous assumption that they learn better younger, is a chief reason for school failure today. It in turn seduces mothers out to the job market, and children are sacrificed. Our offspring simply are not ready for the formal programs of these institutions—especially little boys. Washington State Senator Sam Guess, himself a miller, provides an analogy: "When you grind green grain, you don't get flour. You get gum."[3]

Sense of Rejection

Martin Engel, then head of the U.S. National Early Childhood Demonstration Center, translates institutionalization into parental rejection: "The motive to rid ourselves of our children even if it is partial, is transmitted more vividly to the child [as] rejection which the young child unconsciously senses."[4]

The resulting emptiness and uncertainty set the stage for discouragement and depression. It brings in alien values from other homes to confuse an already threatened nest. Because of your rejection, your child comes to depend on his peers for his values and security. But the values amount to what Cornell's Urie Bronfenbrenner calls "social contagion," as he points out that the peer dependency is already well developed at the preschool level. Little kids have to have designer jeans and the latest running shoes. And they are cruel to those who are not "fortunate" enough to have them.[5]

Furthermore, Bronfenbrenner points out, the peer dependency that comes from closeness to agemates during their first ten or twelve years does not derive so much from the attractiveness of the peers as the disinterest of and perceived rejection by parents. Despite other problems of a Marxist society, it is the greater warmth of Russian parents that makes their fam-

169

ily strength a real challenge to American families—which to-day are considered by some, along with Sweden and England, to be among the coldest, most rejecting in the world.

In the name of history, research, and commonsense, it is time to turn from our bigotry, vested interests, and prejudice against anything that is not conventional . . . and give our children a chance: consider delaying their departure from home. You will lose them soon enough. And even if you keep them longer at home, don't give them formal teaching until at least ages eight or ten.

Dr. Karl Menninger, regarded by many as America's leading authority on mental health, candidly prefers that children, especially boys, remain longer in the home. Even the founding fathers of Head Start now point to the home as the best learning nest. The University of Chicago's Benjamin Bloom adds that parents are not only the best teachers of young children but are also educable.[6] And former Head Start chief psychologist Glen Nimnicht vows that he would prefer to see his grandchildren listening to stories fifteen or twenty minutes a day at home than to let them linger several hours in a preschool.[7]

Add to these views the recent findings that preschool children are fifteen times as likely to be sick as are home-reared youngsters and fifteen times as likely to get involved in negative, aggressive acts, and you have a good reason for emphasizing *home* start.

·······▼▼▼▼▼▼▼▼▼▼▼·· **20** ··▼▼▼▼▼▼▼▼▼▼▼▼▼·····
The Big Tease

I have confessed more than once to being a tease to my little sister, Loraine, and I had my bottom tanned more than once for this crime. I have never made any excuses for such nuisance behavior, although as a psychologist I admit it is tempting. And on mature reflection I now realize it is usually a cowardly act by someone older, bigger, stronger, in a higher position or otherwise advantaged. I am certain now that my parents sometimes were fit to be tied.

Teasing is one of the most common obstacles to discipline in the home and at school. It is usually a selfish or thoughtless act, one without understanding of the needs and maturity of the person teased. By definition it is usually designed to irritate or provoke with petty distractions or annoyances. It is some-times intended as humor, but it is usually not funny, except possibly to the onlooker. The child or adult who teases a younger child is not altogether well adjusted, although hardly a criminal. Much of the time it is a matter of manners. And you *can* do something about it!

Usually teasers will be able to reason enough to have you ask them how they would like to have you tease them in the same way. Or better, suggest that you would like to trust them to take good care of the ones they are teasing. If you remind them that the teaser is usually bigger and stronger than the one teased, you will usually be on the road to a solution. If the teasers are a gang or other group making fun of one person or a minority, this solution still often applies. The Golden Rule usually makes sense to youngsters, once they arrive at or near the age of reason, particularly if you remind them how big or strong they are and show them how they can put their size and strength to better use. *Give them a creative alternative, and work with them.*

We have found that few parents are aware of one of the most serious teasing problems of all: themselves. We have watched parental teasing operate from infancy through adolescence, and upon careful reflection we wonder if we have not done more than our share with our own. Teasing isn't very funny when it involves "that boy" who is your daughter's first heartthrob or when you hold your son in unnecessary doubt about getting the family car or even having a chance to go out. We do not here make a judgment about the car or the date or the heartthrob; we simply suggest that you not trifle with business that is serious to your children. They need understanding much more than teasing.

Kathie Kordenbrock, herself an early childhood specialist and mother of three sons, has this to say about parental teasing:

> As I was sitting in a church nursery with my baby, I was dismayed to see a mother teasing her toddler. She was holding out a toy to the child, then pulling it away just as he reached for it. She finally let him have it when he started screaming. But by then she had him in turmoil, a sort of righteous indignation. Visions of the future welled up in my mind as I watched: How would he treat other children? Or his parents? I truly believe that this mother meant no harm to her child. It was a simple matter of not understanding, of misplaced humor, and of poor child management. She seemed totally unaware of her child's frustration and of the bad behavior she, his parent, was generating. She apparently had no idea of the little fellow's inability to understand her playful motive.

Teasing is common with children, among siblings as well as playmates, yet we are surprised at how many adults seem to

172

use this technique of one-upmanship with children as well as with other adults. Those we have observed seem totally ignorant of the hurt it can cause and usually do it "only in fun." But teasing can be not only belittling to the victim but also in a real sense dishonest. Often we hear erroneous statements or exaggerations made in a mocking way to the chagrin and often embarrassment of the teased.

Many adults, and parents in particular, apparently do not realize that there is a difference between teasing or kidding on the one hand and genuine good-natured humor or fun on the other. Humor is more often defined as appreciating or expressing what is funny or amusing or laughably absurd rather than irritating or mocking or poking fun.

When applying the Golden Rule, we must remember not only to do to others as we would prefer that they do to us, but also to realize that they may have problems that we do not have and that *the Golden Rule may mean something else to them*.

For example, Dorothy likes to have me massage her feet. Therefore should she rub my feet? Hardly. I don't care to have my feet manipulated. But I do like to have her scratch my back. In principle we practice the Golden Rule. To do to others as you would have them do to you is always true in principle, but not always true in method. In other words, be thoughtful. Someone might make a crack about my weight, and I would understand it as humor. But such a remark made about an obese or sensitive friend might bring quite different reactions.

On the other hand, you and I should educate our children to see the bright and happy side whenever we can. Humor should be cultivated and encouraged as much as teasing should be discouraged. Our grandson Brent, then age three, liked peanut butter so much that one day I called him "peanut butter." Just awakened from his nap before lunch, he wasn't ready to be called anything and emitted no more than a grouchy grunt. So I turned away from him to his big brother Bryon, six, and asked what he would like to be called. It so happened that Dorothy had promised a special dessert "for good boys" made out of frozen bananas she had whizzed up with raspberries. Immediately he answered, "I'm banana ice cream," and laughed. Not to be outdone, Brent immediately said, "I'm peanut butter." To this day they happily answer to "Peanut Butter" and "Banana Ice Cream."

For children of all ages, example is the best teacher, although you will do well to explain the basic "whys"—the principles relating to teasing—as your children become mature enough to understand. For children who can read, we have found that a dictionary exercise can be effective. Have them look up the different words, including *humor* and *teasing,* and synonyms which are in most dictionaries. Make a constructive game out of it, not only for your family, but for occasions when their friends, relatives, or neighbors are gathered around your patio or hearth. Also, if you encourage compassion through visiting those who are less fortunate than you and your family and if you otherwise are constructive citizens in the community, much of the temptation to tease, whether selfish or thoughtless, will fade away.

And there will be more happy little sisters!

Discouragement and Depression

I n the October 1984 *Reader's Digest,* Norman Lobsenz tells about "Questions People Ask Ministers Most." One of these is a concern that comes to us daily either by mail, telephone, or visit. "What can I do when I am so discouraged I feel like giving up?" Some of our inquiries are from parents who are at their wit's end or are tired out from trying to "keep ahead of my kids." Others are from mothers, and sometimes dads, who sense that their youngsters are discouraged or pressured by their peers in ways they cannot handle.

Still others are from children. Drugs, alcohol, sex, depression, or other bizarre tastes or behavior take over an otherwise good family and a sensible parent or child. Whatever the age—adult or child—the principles are the same: discouragement and depression threaten all of us when we do not understand their cause. And children, especially young children, are even less likely to understand the "whys." They are the most vulnerable of all.

There are many symptoms of insecure, discouraged, depressed, or even despairing youngsters.

1. *Hyperactivity.* Some are hyperactive, jumping unreasonably all over the place, never relaxing for a minute. This especially is seen among children who have been institutionalized too early. In our book *Home Spun Schools,* we tell the story of the Schaefer family. Jonathan, eight, was nervous and insecure at the classroom demands placed upon him before he was ready. His condition would likely have been worse if he had been fed a poor diet, such as too much protein or sugar or

fat, or ate between meals. His mother settled him down in a week or two by taking him out of school, having him work *with* her around the house, and letting him know he was appreciated. In two weeks he was well settled.

2. *Withdrawal.* Some children will react exactly the opposite from home or school pressures or impatience and will withdraw. Mark Schaefer, eleven, was Jonathan's opposite: seriously withdrawn. His parents, Marge and Dick, also took him out of school and worked closely with him, doing things with him and appreciating him. His uncle also cooperated, teaching him to repair mobile homes. But for withdrawers like Mark it usually takes a little longer. Mark was well in six months.

In *Home Style Teaching,* you will find the story of Matthew, whose working mother found him curled up, uncommunicative on the living room floor. First she tried a competent psychiatrist; then she took him out of school and spent a lot of time doing things with him.

3. *Sluggish and Indifferent.* These youngsters are often tired of school and tired around the house. Many children enrolled in school at five or six are "burned-out" by the third or fourth grade. They, like all others, should have the benefit of careful medical examinations, preferably by reputable pediatricians or family practice physicians. It may be that the youngsters are not in good health. Or their programs—eating, exercising—may not be regular and sound. If these factors are all in order, you likely have a burned-out child. This is a common characteristic of eight- to twelve-year-olds these days who have gone to preschool, kindergarten, or regular school too early.

If you are unable to be your children's comrade during the day, and other members of the family are not available—grandparents, aunts, uncles—do all you can to spend *every* spare minute with them in mornings and evenings. Fathers will be making no sacrifice when they give up the evening paper and television to spend listening time and project periods with their boys and girls.

Back off from heavy formal programs of study; balance their study with hands-on work at home or with Dad on the job. Take them into family business planning, including management of family finance. This will make them feel needed, wanted, and depended on and will allay discouragement and depression.

4. *Stubbornness and Impatience*. Children who put their own priorities ahead of yours and your family's will be helped by the same therapy as those who are sluggish and tired. Apart from regularity and rest, they particularly need the systematic experience of doing things for others, at home, in hospitals, in retirement centers, or in other similar activities. This will help them see the world through others' eyes, and will generate compassion more than selfishness. And your discipline problems will be reduced.

5. *Imagined Needs*. Your children may become depressed at not having all the "things" that other kids have. These are very real wants, but are usually only imagined needs, particularly among peer-dependent kids. Here again you are the best solution, the best distraction. Keep them centered on constructive activities—preferably using their hands and helping others, including you. Many parents have seen their offsprings' selfishness turn to happy, industrious behavior by beginning the simplest of cottage industries and services in which they eventually employ brothers and sisters or other agemates in simple money-earning and neighbor-pleasing activities.

6. *Hostile or Rebellious Behavior*. The first thing to check here is usually your own behavior. Assuming that careful medical tests have been made, including, if necessary, scans for possible brain tumors or other damage, ask yourself some questions: Do I yell around the house? Do I act rebellious to my spouse? Children? Employer? Neighbors? Or am I gentle, deliberate, restrained?

177

All children—and spouses—need emotional support. Some need more than others. Yet don't assume that your louder, more aggressive child will need any less attention and appreciation and companionship than the others. Indeed, such children, properly guided, may become your closest and best helpers in rearing your others and in "keeping" your home.

7. *Psychosis*. For children whose depression has reached beyond your ability to cope, see your family physician. But make sure that your professional help stands for exemplary values and has *spiritual* understanding that meshes with your ideals. While we have our own clear preferences, we do not distinguish here among Catholic, Protestant, Mormon, Muslim, or Jew. Psychology has gone full cycle in the last two or three generations. Students of the mind are once again opening their own minds to the healing beliefs in a higher power.

More and more psychologists are daring to introduce God into the sanctuary of professional psychological associations. More and more are admitting to the cleansing therapy of guilt and grace. Dr. William Wilson, emeritus professor of psychiatry at Duke University Medical School, has told of his 90 percent recovery rate among mental patients who develop a sound religious faith. And many psychiatrists agree. Even thirty-five years ago a secular practitioner, Dr. J. T. Fisher, then considered by many to be dean of American psychiatrists, declared that Christ's Sermon on the Mount was better than the sum of all books on mental health and was phrased in language more beautiful than that "of the most capable of living poets."[1] If ever there was a place for the assurance that "prayer changes things," it is here.

Those Special Children: Adopted, Foster, or Step

With millions of families unsettled from alarming increases in divorce, some parents and children are unsure how much loyalty or affection they dare invest in family members. An entirely new disciplinary situation has fogged the family scene. Modern society is laying on many of our children behavior burdens that are no fault of their own. Stepchildren, adoptees, and foster care kids are no longer rare breeds and may soon outnumber their whole-family friends. A problem that was once unique has turned into a common one which must be faced.

It surely is one of the most challenging dilemmas in family discipline today and affects even families which are not themselves divided, because of their relationships with relatives and friends from broken homes. As almost any of these "special" children can tell you, most of the people who study them do not understand their problems, unless *they have been stepchildren,* too. But before long, the way things are going, most specialists will themselves have come from broken families.

This is not to say that all foster or step or adoptee homes are bad. Some of them are among the finest, most loving, and stable families we know. Nor are "whole" families always exempt from poor behavior. Some may even be worse. Joyce Forrest of Crossroads, a Cleveland, Ohio, halfway house, tells us how her parents were alcoholics, fighting so much that she hid under the bed. Although the family was "whole," her mother was so desperate she tried to give Joyce away. But there were no takers. On the other hand, when she was eventually shunted to foster care, one of her foster mothers locked her in the cellar overnight, killed her dog—her one living friend—and made her watch while she burned the toys Joyce's father had sent. It might be added here that random use of foster care is one of the most brutal, abusive tools that judges and thoughtless social workers use in making the cure worse than the disease.

It takes strong, balanced, loving adults with high values to be worthy foster or step or adopting parents. As I grew older, I saw this more and more in my second mother. The Talmud says it well:

> A mother is likened unto a mountain spring,
> That nourishes the tree at the root,
> But one who mothers another's child
> Is likened unto a water that rises into a cloud
> And goes a long distance, to nourish a lone tree in the
>   desert.

All children deserve love. These special children should never be treated as discards, as they are often considered to be. They deserve our deepest understanding and most extended patience, whether we are their parents, relatives, neighbors, or friends. Circumstances have betrayed them; but let us not betray them anew. Often those of us not in the family can do more for these special youngsters through appropriate warmth, understanding, and encouragement than their parents can.

I speak from a stepchildhood which knew the uncertainties both of such children and adults, and Dorothy and I have some idea of the extra effort that successful foster parents are compelled to make, for we have had the precious and enlightening experience of helping to raise the children of many other parents—youngsters who became as our own. We often found ourselves falling short in a relationship that requires a compassion which few adults apparently know and sacrifice which few are prepared to make, except for money. Although we were never paid, we have asked ourselves many times if we were worthy.

One of our special children was at first near suicide from rejection by her own father. Another, naturally brilliant, was ill-prepared for school because of family complexities and had to be given very basic help in her studies without giving her the impression that she was "dumb"—as she insisted she was.

On still other occasions we would receive a late night call from the police inquiring if we were the parents of a child they picked up at two in the morning out walking the streets. We would go downtown and retrieve our treasure and work harder than ever to provide the right kind of affection and security and help the otherwise helpless to overcome his or her past.

Still another was a prepubescent girl addicted to masturbation. She was Dorothy's project, but we all loved her. She grew up—as all of our girls did—to become a worthy wife and mother. I do, however, add a word of caution here. A father must be careful to avoid even the appearance of inappropriate gestures of affection. If his mind is on the welfare of his children, he will have little or no trouble with this. The same applies to women and boys, although the problem here is less likely and therefore less frequent.

Today the nature of the problems of such special youngsters has been complicated far beyond the needs of the step children of two or three generations ago. Most divided homes were then the result of a mother's or daddy's death. They are now more often the events of divorce or (unmarried) liaisons or parental incompetence or rejection, a much more complex façade for children to face. Their parents are still living, usually in anger or indifference, frequently preferring the overtures of a new lover to the affection of their spouse and kids.

Yet there are times when the fault should not be laid on

either parents or children. Some divisions have been engineered by in-laws. Some have been created by well-meaning pastors, lawyers, physicians, professional counselors, and others. Some result from circumstances which seem beyond anybody's control.

For better or worse, children often do not have the benefit of either family, but are given over to foster care or random rearing by relatives or others. These youngsters are cast in an even more difficult role than adopted children. It is usually much easier and more convincing to be able to tell children that they have been "chosen" than to have to admit to them that they are victims of circumstances or awards of the court. So renew the "choosing" every day!

On the other hand children who are adopted into *whole* families tend, as they grow older, to reason with some consistency and realize that they were really chosen. This has particular meaning when they find that some natural children were "accidents" and their parents did not really want them. To be chosen begins to mean that they are *special*.

Nor will there be much talk among stepfamilies in which one parent has brought children to the marriage and the other spouse has brought none, unless both parents are especially considerate of each other and involve the offspring as partners in family dialogue and planning.

For foster youngsters and families where both widowed or divorced parents have brought their offspring to a common home, there is likely to be much more talk, and unless this is lovingly monitored, there may be confusion and even antagonism. Occasionally there may be little or no talk at all. That is the more to be feared. We should keep our channels open and clear.

Foster children and those of mixed families are generally curious about how others like them have fared. "Did you live with your mother or your dad?" they will ask another foster child in their home. It hardly occurs to some of them that there is such a thing as a whole family. Their questions may reflect a simple curiosity or be an outreach for companionship which they need at the moment. Yet they may later feel that they have to defend their questions and answers, whether right or wrong. They are often unsettled, insecure.

"How often do you see your dad?" or "Does he ever come to see you?" or "How do you like it here?" are also common and natural questions among foster children. Their preoccupation with how others are treated by adults frequently overrides their recollections or curiosities about how their parents treated each other.

Yet occasionally such memories can become quite frank and even terrifying in their recital. Whether or not we are a part of these happenings, almost all of us have nearby friends who are, and it becomes us to be compassionate, appreciative, encouraging neighbors both to parents and children. Oftentimes we can turn the tide for some—children or parents—who are discouraged, simply by helping them to know that they are valued.

Stepchildren usually have at least one parent, and that can either be a great advantage or become deeply confusing, sometimes sooner, sometimes later. Let's consider one of the mildest of cases we know.

A Case History

We have a dear friend and counselor who was a stepson, but he was not the product of divorce, so did not have to choose between his own father and another dad. He did not have to hug and kiss both his own mother and a new mother as children of divorce are often required to do. His loyalties were not torn so that he could not give honest answers to common questions and still survive. He did not live for a week or a month or a year with one set of parents and one set of values and then move over to another home a mile or a thousand miles away where the values were even further apart.

183

For these and other reasons, divorce is often worse than death.

In this case our friend was a stepchild in western New York whose widowed father had remarried. And in my counseling with him through the years from his childhood, I found that he developed a greater awareness than many adults that the discipline—or discipleship—of such youngsters involves some quite different behavior problems than are found among children of complete families. We present this case study *from his viewpoint as a child:*

His mother died when he was five years old and his little sister was less than two. His mother had often risked her own health by helping her neighbors and caring for her family through two epidemics which had destroyed people all around her. Relatives and friends told stories for years of the remarkable beauty of person and character of this woman. She was known in the community as "that angel," giving of herself wherever and whenever there was a call—from the nearby Indian tribes, Mexicans, or the charities of the little Lutheran church where she and his father were lay leaders and which was the social center of their lives.

Several years after she died, his father moved to another state to go into business. It was an unsettling time for the two young ones and filled with excitement as they first lived in campers, then shacks, then built a house, with their brave grandma, who had taken over when their mother died, and their very special father, setting the pace for all. For a few years their father remained single as he built up a profitable business, and like any kids who are not alert to adult affairs, they had little idea of what was going on when, after five years, their father was gone evening after evening for months. Then suddenly this pretty young woman moved in with them, and their revered grandma moved out. At their age they had little concept of marriage.

All seemed to go well, except that their new mother was

merely that nice lady in church as far as they were concerned. Although theirs had been an affectionate family with much kissing and embracing, it was now hard to learn to hug and to kiss her, nice as she was. Boys just don't kiss ladies in the church unless they have a crush on them. Before long this brother and sister began feeling that their dad liked her better than he did them.

In their childish ways, this brother and sister reasoned more from what their father did not do, than from what their new mother did do. He did not spend so much story time as before and was not quite so regular in tucking them in bed. And their new mother had little experience in this direction—as if she were uncomfortable doing it. The inevitable alienation growing out of this parental inexperience or thoughtlessness developed an insecurity in them which they still feel today, although their new mother had apparently shown no hostility to them. The problem was that she had not done enough to endear them.

With that record in child care, she proceeded to give birth to a baby girl, a cute little thing, and all were proud. The only problem was that they now seemed one more step away from their father who had been their main "security blanket." And if the truth were known, they were one step further from seeing him as their model.

Then she had another daughter. Now the children were two and two, except that it seemed as if every spare moment of the older youngsters was taken up doing chores for their mother and *her* kids. To make room for the new arrivals, the older children had been relegated to a little patched-on room built for them behind the bathroom at the back of the house. It was actually cute, but it was isolated and emotionally cold, separating them further from the rest of the family. Its one redeeming feature was that it did give them some time to themselves. Yet that isolation only bred further doubt and alienation.

And lastly, from their viewpoint—which may not have been at all fair—it seemed that they were cowering under their step-mother for fear that she might report to their dad their every misdemeanor of the day—which she did frequently. It seemed to their young minds that she regarded her two as nearly perfect and her stepchildren as in her way, except as they might be useful to her. These feelings of alienation and hostility stayed with them into early adulthood when they finally began to see how things might have looked through her eyes—a friendly church member who accepted the mothering of two stepragamuffins. Thus the state of stepparenthood is not one to be envied.

But neither is the status of stepchildren, although this family never used that term. Some lessons can be learned. Stepparents should consider these alternatives:

1. Take your children into your planning even beyond normal constraints and even to courtship or marriage activity insofar as the reasoning of children permits. Do things with them, appointing them as officers in a family business even if it is so simple as gardening and selling produce or mowing lawns for the neighbors.

2. Preserve every worthwhile tie with the past, including frequent visits with grandparents and other relatives.

3. See that stepchildren get special attention from their own parent if that is possible. This can usually be done in all but foster and adoptive situations, at least so that they do not feel shoved aside, with all the insecurity this almost always brings.

4. In no way allow them to seem demeaned, for example, by putdowns on things they can't control (size, age, color) or by ridicule or by indifference to their questions.

5. Do not force the child to display affection to the new parent or parents, but let adults earn it by genuine love—surprises under the children's pillows or special campouts. And pray for wisdom and help, which in some cases can come only from God.

6. Don't allow or provide for any separation or isolation

that is not absolutely necessary: Don't take out members from one side of the family to the exclusion of the other without logical reason. Never show partiality of any kind.

7. Insure that the stepparents are never in a perpetual position of reporting on those who are not really their own. Instead the stepparent should do everything possible to deserve the children's trust and affection.

8. Practice more holding, touching, and other assurances of genuine affection as appropriate, insuring that no gestures are made which might suggest undue intimacy, as for example, a stepfather with a budding stepdaughter. (See also chapter 9 on "Warm Responsiveness and Example.")

These points are particularly true for children who have not yet arrived at the age of consistent reasonability. When they reach the age of eight or ten to twelve, depending on their maturity, they should be treated as full partners in the family, with virtually all plans open to their survey, decision-sharing, and, if possible, participation.

This leads us to what will be standard therapy by the time you read this book, and it was here that the father in this model family excelled. He took an interest in the older children as the years moved on. During periods when they were not in school, he took them with him on the job. This was a lifesaver. Their dad also saw that they had increasing authority and freedom on the job as they proved themselves in responsibility and skill. Such day-long experience with a father can be a great healer, particularly where the stepparent is the mother. Yet every effort should also be made for them to have an element of independence, even if it is only babysitting for another family or house cleaning for neighbors.

Although we had unusually happy experiences, we found that even with our foster children some of them occasionally disobeyed or were indifferent. They are not to be specially indulged but made to feel responsible, accountable—no different from any other family members.

And a word to adopted children and to foster children like ours for whose care we expected no pay: you are more special than most children because you were specifically chosen. And you should sense this. Our special children are now more "family" to us than most blood children today.

Mothers and fathers and brothers and sisters have much to give to these special children. Our blood children, Dennis and Kathie, were always consulted and always had a part in choosing our special children. Don't let your neglect or inconsistency get in the way. If ever example is important, it is with these children. Place yourselves in their place, and plan to take them with you when possible. Yet realize one possibility that always lingers around the corner. There are some children who will never respond; it is not in their genes to respond, or alienating influences have gotten to them before you got there.

But if you give them yourselves, concentrating more on work and service than on sports and amusements, you will likely do well. Fix their bicycle tires *with* them. Wash the car *with* them. Trim the lawn *with* them. Plan a party *with* them. Go camping *with* them instead of taking them to spectator events. See that they are *doing,* not just *looking;* that they are *involved,* not only *interested.* And you will be their heroes and heroines rather than their ogres. Yours will be one *special* family!

·······················23·······················

Those Unique Children: The Handicapped

When Dorothy organized and directed the cerebral palsy center at a major medical school, she found that many of these spastic children seemed even quicker mentally than the average normal child. It may be that she loved them so much that she was prejudiced. Yet love and mental competence go closely together, and spastic children are often among our brightest.

Love can also do remarkable things for seriously retarded children. One of the most urgently needed lessons of my life was taught me by my brother Charles and his wife Doris, a nurse. Their son, Larry, was born so severely retarded that some physicians and psychologists assumed that his reasoning ability would never rise above that of a two- or three-year-old. Trained typically in the university classes of the 1930s and 1940s, I assumed that the best care for him would be the California State Home for Retarded Children at Sonoma, and so advised.

"No," Charles told me firmly. "We will take care of him."

I reminded him of the restrictions of such a life of care, of the expense, and of their own lack of specialization in the area of retardation.

"We love him," was Charles' answer, "and we'll make out somehow."

And make out they did, utilizing all the resources of the community, friends, nearby college, and even some of us who did not approve. In the next years we learned a lot of lessons about love and its therapy for the handicapped. We learned among other things that a child may be seriously handicapped in reasoning, but may have remarkable talents in other areas. We learned that even the amount of patience and care that one would give a favorite pet can produce significant results in a retarded child, whatever the psychology buffs advise.

Returning from the Orient a few years after Larry's birth, we were astonished and delighted that this severely retarded child, with extremely limited reasoning, was helpful around the house. More amazingly to us, he could play both the piano and electric organ well. He did a remarkably good job on the cello, and his teachers had found that he was endowed with perfect pitch! Most of all, it dawned on us that he had a special capacity for love: he was an outgoing, affectionate boy who would embrace you at the suggestion of a smile.

Sue was and is a Down's syndrome child. Fifty to seventy-five years ago psychologists would have called her a "Mongolian idiot." But, as we implied above, psychologists can change their minds. In fact modern psychology, for all the foolishness that some of it has generated, has done a remarkable job in showing what can be done with a Down's youngster. Most practitioners would be angry or dismayed if some one suggested today that these precious youngsters are idiots.

Sue, like nearly all the Down's children that we have known, is a naturally happy, loving, gentle child, willing to do anything she can to help her parents and anyone else around her. Her unselfish nature should be the envy of normal children. Her parents first taught her basic discipline and response. Then they moved on to educate her to be the homemaker's assistant, the associate car washer, and an absolutely terrific garden weeder.

Some of these very special children will, of course, require much more care than others, particularly those who cannot get around by themselves. Most, if not all, of them will take longer than others to learn bladder and bowel control, how to eat by themselves, and how to dress themselves. Some may never be able to tie their shoes and button their clothes. Some, spastic or paralyzed, may need complete custodial care. Let's make sure that it is wholehearted as with the possession of great treasure.

Parents of such children must be firm in training their young ones. They should not worry much about what their visitors think. Often they may have to repeat their instructions, quietly as possible, and still see no positive response. For the good of all, circumstances may force them to guide these children to another room—not because they feel ashamed, but for their children's own good and for the progress of the party or dinner or conversation. Yet they should never betray a self-consciousness about their children's differences. In fifty years of professional life, we know of only one or two homes in which, for example, Down's children or spastic children were not appreciated for the promising and helpful youngsters that they can be, nearly all of whom demonstrate some kind of genius.

More than almost any other children, handicapped youngsters thrive on routine. This should be established and continued from their earliest days and years. Creative opportunities should be provided for all—picnics, nature watching—but especially for those who are handicapped only in body, but not in mind. Professional, clinical help should be sought for these youngsters, but even the quality of this aid should be measured at least in part by the affection these specialists show for the child.

Specialists can provide counsel on activities for these special children. For example, many Down's youngsters are highly useful around the kitchen and can be taught to be careful around heat and electricity and gas. A Down's boy of a neighbor of ours in Michigan kept their gardens nicely weeded and the lawn mowed. In fact some of these youngsters will work better by themselves than normal kids.

We don't suggest extremes, but drop the hint that most

handicapped children—including the blind, deaf, and spastic—are generally underchallenged. They, like normal people, like to feel as normal as possible, and this feeling is best cultivated by helping them to be useful. Keep them on the stretch rather than unnecessarily indulging them. It is you who will make the difference between happiness and boredom by working *with* them and learning what you can from specialists.

In your efforts to provide recreation—reading, listening, manual activities—we again stress the importance of providing books and tapes and things which are natural and true. It does no harm to let them have stories of other handicapped people like Helen Keller and Joni Erickson-Tada. Let them know that they are valued for the lift that their spirits and, where possible, their help gives you.

Whenever it can be provided, then, remember that handicapped children, of all children, need the security of their homes, if their homes are worthy at all. These children are unique, and often their very handicaps will bring out a special creative brilliance. If they are vision or hearing impaired, you will do well to learn Braille or signing. If they need physical therapy, learn to provide as much of it as you can at home. But most of all, make it a rule to be generous in patience, understanding, and love.

24

Letting Boys Become Men and Girls Become Women

Boys simply do not develop like girls. This can stir up disciplinary dilemmas that will turn your hair gray if you do not have some idea about how their differences are likely to affect you, your children, and even your society. Boys in their early years do get in Mother's hair far more often than girls, so at the risk of some repetition and stirring up some of your conventional ideas, we will give them their day in court.

One of the most serious obstacles to family harmony and sensible child behavior and control, especially *self-control*, is the difference in relative maturity between boys and girls. Yet the basic reason for serious problems in most cases is simply that parents give little or no attention to these differences because they either do not know or don't care. Let's look at a "for instance":

My young friends, Jake, from Forest Falls, California; Mark, from Fort Wayne, Indiana; and Tony, from Queens, New York, all have several things in common. They started school very early; they burned out from school pressures; their parents were too busy with sports, work, and TV; and they face a world that is, to say the least, hostile to boys. All three were learning-failed, two were acutely hyperactive, and one was seriously withdrawn. Compounding this, Jake's and Mark's mothers were working full-time, and Tony's mother was working part-time out of the home. We say "out of home" because we believe that full-time mothering is also a full-time job. All three mothers said they worked because they "needed fulfillment." This is a great risk when you have boys.

These are boys who want to be men, but who will never get there if we don't stop putting them down. Thirteen boys to every girl fidget in special education classes for those who are "failing." Eight boys to each girl waste away in sessions for the emotionally ill!

America once was a man's country, and boys wanted to be men, although, of course, wherever you have real men you also have very special women. But it seems today that some females are trying hard to out-male them and in many respects are succeeding. Ultimately this will hurt our women even more than the men. And all of us must share the praise or blame: men, women, and our schools.

Men First in Accountability

Woman has always been special in the male American's dream. He has not seen her as the ravening wolf Carl Jung described to Sigmund Freud. The macho man pictured her as sweet, demure, winsome, wide-eyed, wholesome, and even naive. When he married her, he took for granted that she would be a good cook and the best of mothers and that she would care for him. This was old-fashioned family discipline at its best—not perfect bliss, but remarkable unity and security, with few divided families.

Unfortunately, as our nation prospered, technology arrived, and we moved more and more from a rural to an urban and suburban society, man often forgot that caring is a two-way street. He might have known, if we are to believe the creation story, that he was created first so that he could nurture the one who would carry his child. He might have reasoned, whether religious or not, just on the basis of commonsense, that if he is to be head *of* the home, he must also be the example *for* the home—in patience, kindness, forgiveness, and love. If he expects to have 51 percent of the authority, he must accept 51 percent of the responsibility in demonstrating these graces, for

194

authority must always be kept commensurate with responsibility in any viable organization, most of all in a family. Parental self-discipline is the best predictor of family discipline.

Once upon a time a gentleman would lay down his coat so his lady would not dirty her pretty feet. He carried her across a puddle to guard her long skirt and shoes. He walked on the curb side on the street to protect her from the splashes of passing cars. He opened and closed the door of her taxi and ushered her first out of the elevator and into the office. He even gave her his seat on the streetcar or bus.

But boys seldom see this anymore, much less do it. Without caring males for examples, boys don't know how to be complete men.

My father, though not college educated, insisted that his sons learn and abide by these courtesies. To this day we are conscience-stricken if we don't. Except for the first—laying our coats in the puddle as Sir Walter Raleigh did so that our women would not get their dainty feet wet—we learned that women must be treated as "first, last, and best."

I am grateful to Dorothy that for over forty-eight years she has made the second easier by keeping a trim figure. But whether our women are old or young, thin or fat, we have no excuse for not giving them our seats in buses or opening doors for them or granting them deferential treatment wherever we go. It is great to see that some men—and boys—still do it. But most do not. . . .

Women's Unique Role

Into this vacuum of male models enter women who call themselves feminists, because in part men have demanded too much and given too little. And to that extent, they are not to be blamed.

Their more radical types apparently don't aspire to be womanly, but rather insist on being treated like men. They want no

195

special courtesies, no tender care—again robbing the male of one of his unique roles. Some frankly suggest that down under their lipstick, mascara, and rouge throbs an eagerness for maleness, which thrives on hostility to the very gender they envy. Yet we believe that most normal women still desire caring, nurturing males who respect them and listen to them as having wisdom from a unique—feminine—point of view.

Of course, in many homes women are forced to assume the spiritual, emotional, and financial leadership roles their husbands have abandoned or ignored. Many women shrink from, or actually resent, having these husbandly responsibilities in addition to their conventional burdens as mothers and wives. They still do not like to be treated like men; they prize their larger responsibility of personally nurturing their young.

In many of our homes, these women clearly reign, but they operate in such a way that we, their men, don't really know it. Even when women do assume some of the man's authority, the most successful ones make it appear that the man is in control. They seem proud to be women—not to be dominated, but cared for, protected.

Disruptive feminism has emerged after virtually all of history's great wars. When men returned from battle, women had to leave the factories and their wartime "freedom" from their children. During the Grecian wars, women were forced to leave their young ones in the hands of the slaves. So also in Rome and during the French Revolution. By World War II we called it "day care."

After a few generations without parental precepts and examples, there were no family values to pass on; the Grecian and Roman families collapsed, and society with them. Harvard sociologist Carle Zimmerman offers one notable difference from the United States today: Rome and Greece had strong familial nations waiting to take over. American civilization has no such prospect. Whether the historian is Sandburg

196

or Gibbon, whether the country be America or Rome, the prior rights of the family must be absolute. Based on family trends, Dr. Zimmerman sees the end of a free America, perhaps before the end of this century.[1]

Cornell family psychologist Urie Bronfenbrenner—no Communist himself—sees Russia as a world power whose family closeness is stronger than ours. Russia's vow, of course, is to repeat history. This assumes erosion from within more than attack from without.

In many respects the center of today's world political drama is the family, and the most vulnerable unit of the family is the boy. Talk to these youngsters and see how they feel about women. Caught between their growing male egos and the demands of awakened females, they falter at defining their roles.

After all, men can't give birth. They can't nurse babies. They can't even make milk. On the other hand, no matter how restless women may be, men are not prepared to be replaced. Boys, creators of our society's most numerous disciplinary problems, are caught in the middle of this combination of ignorance, dereliction, and calculation.

Unfortunately, teachers also put boys down quite regularly, as government studies show, even though they eventually perform quite comparably with girls. When mothers learn of these teacher estimates, unlike Mrs. Edison with her young son Tom, they often assume that the teacher is right, and their boys are not very bright or not well behaved. They directly or by attitude communicate this unfair indictment as accusation to their offspring, with almost certain guarantee of disappointment, frustration, and eventually disrespect and disciplinary problems.

What chance do boys—and men—have when feminists assume unreasonably that all men are like the worst of their male companions and that today's boys will be worse? They are insuring the fulfillment of their own prophecies. One feminist says she has a feeling of hatred that moves her to a "castration fantasy" where she slaughters [men] in her "fury." Boys—and men—are mystified and alarmed.

Although "those kinds" of feminists, we believe, are a scant minority, they efficiently secure a lioness's share of federal and private funds to advance their network goals. They and their supporters, many of them male, deliberately or ignorantly do not like little boys. They use their taxpayer-financed funds to control the future of young males. And since boys become men, feminists often have society—the rest of us—stepping to their beat.

Our Schools

History and research clearly show that over the last half century we have by accident and design barred our boys from success both at home and at school. We have diluted their uniqueness in the military and the work place—and in the home. We could not have done a more effective job of creating disciplinary problems if we had planned with great calculation. On one pretext or another we have pushed boys out of the home long before they are ready. We demand that they compete with girls, even though we know very well that when they start school, boys are about a year less mature, and few can keep up.

The girls have had it bad enough. As they, like the boys, have been rushed into school earlier and earlier, they have become less competent in learning, behavior, and social skills. Now more and more of them, too, are found in the realm of the uncontrolled. In these fast-moving times with their worldly-wisdom and absence of time to develop in balance, their physical maturity comes sooner for both girls and boys, but their senses, reasoning abilities, and brain development have not kept pace. They are unbalanced kids, like little sheep whose *shepherds* have gone astray.

John Dewey warned nearly a hundred years ago that age

eight is "early enough for anything more than an incidental attention to visual and written language form."[2] And his advice is strikingly supported by replicable research today. We daily disable our children by public policy and then ask for tax money to remedy our dereliction. In the last generation we built up a remarkable new profession of *special education* to carry this out.

Tufts University learning psychologist David Elkind warns that early formal schooling is *burning out* our children. University of California's William Rohwer agrees. Cornell family specialist Urie Bronfenbrenner found that children who are with their peers more than their parents at least until the fifth or sixth grades—about ages eleven or twelve—will become peer dependent. These youngsters knuckle under to the rivalry, ridicule, habits, manners, and values of their agemates. And to the extent that they are so influenced, they lose four crucial assets: self-worth, optimism, respect for parents, and even trust in their peers.

These youngsters are *negatively* socialized—captives of the narcissistic trends of the day. These well-established findings and those of the Smithsonian research precisely contradict our common assumptions that our children need much association with other children in order to be socialized.

But the loss has been much greater for boys than for girls, and they get into trouble several times as often. Government studies in the 1970s found that boys tended to be rated lower than girls in intellectual ability and academic performance, though their actual performance was about the same.[3] This should not surprise us, for the little guys are obviously less mature, more likely to be hyperactive, and generally more troublesome to teachers and less ready for formal learning. The situation requires an unusual teacher, one who understands the developmental needs of children, especially little boys, and who does not lop all of them into the same garbage pile, simply because they are not yet ripe.

Boys who are considered to be slow learners are not accepted socially. This may give us one of many reasons why learning failure and delinquency go together.[4]

Solutions

Happily, mothers and fathers and teachers and lawyers and judges and legislators of most states are beginning to look at history and research with commonsense. They are slowing the onslaught of the state, insuring that parents have a larger control and that children are allowed to mature longer in the family nest.

A powerful home-school renaissance is exciting hundreds of thousands of families from coast to coast and is reaching overseas from Europe to Australia and Japan. Its origins are as old as history, and it echoes the American heritage, which gave us home-taught kids that became national heroes. Both boys and girls do quite well at home when mothers and fathers are warm and responsive, regardless of the level of the parents' education.

Home-schooling parents average between two and three years of college and range from Alaska backwoodsmen to White House officials, including hundreds of physicians, attorneys, legislators, judges, sports heroes, ministers, and teachers as well as both public and church school administrators, psychologists, and guidance counselors. Among them are a presiding family court judge of Indianapolis and world class miler Jim Ryun. And they are widely supported by pediatricians, some of whom have left their practices to stay home and teach their kids.

As I write this paragraph, a Portland, Oregon, Montessori teacher called, troubled by the needs of her six-year-old boy who is in first grade in a public school. She has not yet read the things we have given you in this book, but as a true professional, who is more concerned with children than the pursuit of the dollar, she is making plans to quit her job next year and spend time with her boys, ages six and three, at home.

Little boys are not little men. They need time to grow naturally and to stabilize their values before they are institutionalized. A little chicken is more self-sufficient six minutes after it is born than a child is after six years of life, yet we would not take it away from its nest.

Those who worry that home-cared children will not be sufficiently socialized should look at research and at today's children. They might also consider the values most of them learn in today's schools—a more serious problem than learning failure.

So often, we unthinkingly bow to convention and rush our little human beings out of home into institutions without sound reasons. We raise a clamor about the desperate straits of our schools, yet the solution is to a large degree in our hands. Let institutions have their day. For those youngsters who cannot have Mother at home, we must provide better, more homelike, institutional care. Let the home provide the school the foundation—the mature youngsters—it so badly needs today. I am glad to report that the working mothers of Jake, Mark, and Tony, one of them a single parent, have all given up their jobs out of home and are doing well, very well with their boys. This is not always possible, but every effort should be made to make it so.

Contrary to scare talk that such children are being held captive by narrow-minded or abusive parents, researchers have found that home-taught youngsters excel in achievement, behavior, and social perception. Home scholars average about 30 percent higher on standardized tests than do classroom students. We determined this by obtaining the standardized achievement test scores of children whose parents had been threatened or taken to court. These averaged 80.1 percent as compared with 50 percent, which is the average for classroom-taught youngsters. None of these parents were considered well-to-do and most of them were high-school educated. There is, of course, good reason for this record: the one-to-one tutorial method, which has never been surpassed. But whether or not you educate your children formally at home, make sure that by precept and example you give them the most important education of all: creative minds, noble spirits, and honest souls.

If there is anything historians agree upon, it is a nation's dependence upon its family for survival. Whether Sandburg or Gibbon, whether America or Rome, there is no substitute for virile family strength.

Girls have it bad enough, but they don't have the handicaps of immaturity and of feminist vitriol that boys face every day. If we want to make our boys into men and our girls into women, if we want self-controlled children, then let us be gentlemen and ladies and builders of homes where our youngsters can grow up without the certainty of being put down. With this male-female balance, and the mothers of Jake, Mark, and Tony enjoying their sons, the hands that rock the cradle still will rule the world. And their men will be proud of it.

Creative Punishment

A friend of ours found her two youngsters, ages four and six, quarreling again one day. But this time she had a plan. Instead of telling them to stop, she asked each of them if he was the problem.

Both answered no.

"Then the *toys* must be naughty!" And her flabbergasted boys watched with anguish as she gently switched the teddy bear and spanked a little truck and put them away "to bed" on a high shelf.

Like any creative work, effective discipline requires some organization, some planning. It pays not only to have a schedule and notes on things to do each day, but also a plan, to devise methods of dealing with situations most likely to arise.

One mother was faced with children who were always playing games with her to get their way—teasing, threatening, cajoling, pretending, persuading, pleading. Finally she decided to start the tape recorder during the next blow-up. When replayed, her young son and daughter quickly got the point. Another time, when trouble broke out at the table, she took their plates to tables in separate rooms, away from the family. Her planning worked.

Another friend of ours held a funeral for toys that were left lying around. She "buried" them out of sight from where they could be resurrected, only one each day, and then only on good behavior. Yet another friend found that her children were quicker to put their toys away after she arranged them out on the living room floor just before their playmates were to arrive.

We insist that *discipline* does not equal *punishment*. Discipline, we believe, is the fine art of discipleship. Our goal is to help children to understand that if they cannot control themselves, they will never be worthy of influencing or controlling others.

Yet there comes a time in nearly all children's lives when you have to "take them in hand." For disgruntled infants this may mean no more at times than checking to see that they are well and secure and then letting them cry it out. A snap on the hand or slap on the bare bottom will do marvels for a child of two or three. And by the time they are beginning to reason a little, deprivation of privileges or things usually has the most salient effect of all. All will be done with your goal of building genuine self-worth.

At whatever age your children are not performing acceptably, take time to use your authority. Do some creative thinking about the *cause* of the problem and possible outcomes. In other words, diagnose the disease rather than treat the symptoms, and then prescribe the cure. For example, if your children are being disrespectful, from whom are they learning this? From their playmates? From other adults? Or even from you? How do you treat your spouse and vice versa? How do you speak to your children? Or how do their friends treat their parents or one another?

Have you consistently and reasonably set their boundaries? If you have not, they will set *yours*, they will train *you*. If they are not your helpers, you will be their slaves. If you do not wisely tighten down on them when necessary, they will tighten down on you. Wise control is firm, almost rigid, in the early years, and gradually lets up as your child becomes more reason-able. Otherwise you may be training a little male chauvinist, jumping at his every demand, and hardly a candidate for sainthood as a husband. Or a daughter who will be so spoiled today that she will be anathema to her husband tomorrow.

Will it help if you lay down an ultimatum that you will not put up with such talk? Perhaps, though you may instill undercover rebellion, which will not surface until later. But if you don't set a consistently sound example and don't treat the cause, the situation will not really be cured. Whatever it is, the conditions need to be adjusted or changed, even an apology and a new determination on your part if your example is at fault. In general, the disciplinary methods or techniques must be altered if the results are not satisfactory.

Corporal Punishment

When and if you are certain that corporal punishment—physical pain—is necessary, undertake it only with love, deliberate planning, and with greatest care. Ask yourself the questions, "Have I been specific in my instruction in this matter? Have I considered my children's ages and maturity levels? Have I been gentle and patient, winning them more than ruling them? Does my life lead them or confuse them?"

Never should you or I treat corporal punishment as a standard solution to our behavior problems. Never should it be done with little thought, impatience, or anger. Before you can control others effectively, you must learn to control yourself. Yet, if you must punish, don't unnecessarily delay.

Some families—Christians, Muslims, Jews—insist that physical discipline should be preceded with prayer. If so, parents should make sure that the children understand, or the prayer will be little more than mockery both to them and their God.

When it is necessary to switch very small children, promptness is important—just as with a puppy that operates more from instinct than from reason. Remember that in their first two or three years your children's brains are not mature enough to respond quickly to verbal commands. When those commands are yells, your children become confused, even depressed. Walk into your closet or the bathroom or any place where you can cool off, but never yell at your child unless in emergency, as near a fire or swimming pool or cliff; even there be sure you don't worsen the situation.

After ages four or five, when reasoning is developing rapidly, whether you pray or not, you will do well nearly always to begin such a corporal session with a well-reasoned conference with the erring children, unless of course they are too immature to be fully reasonable. Some mature much later than others. As we have noted in Part II of this book, some children mature three or four years or more earlier or later than others in one aspect or another of their development.

Deprivation of privileges or favorite foods or cherished new clothes or a bike or other recreational items or use of the family car is better than corporal punishment for most children after eight or ten. This may mean that you, too, will have to sacrifice by staying home from a party or concert or game which you have keenly anticipated, if you have made your children's behavior a condition of family participation.

Consistency here equals honesty and is imperative. But you will find the price well worth paying when your children find that you mean exactly what you say, even if it costs you some sacrifice. *The worst form of parenting, like the worst form of cowardice, is to know what is right and not do it regardless of price.*

In the event spanking or whipping is necessary it should be done with a switch or strap which will not cause serious bodily harm; it should never be done with your hand or foot. And don't be surprised if it raises a minor welt. *This is not child abuse.* But slapping is totally out as a method of punishment. It almost always conveys your loss of control of your own feelings and of the entire situation, and is abusive when done as discipline.

Divided Homes

Children of divorce and other divisions of the home must be handled as firmly as normal children until they are consistently reasonable, but with few exceptions the action should be with the initiation and fullest support of the blood parent and consistent with the highest values of the family. If the provocation is serious enough to reflect both sides of the stepfamily, both, wherever possible, should participate in its resolution. These days such occasions often arise—children into drugs, dropouts from school, sexual experimentation, pregnancies, and like dilemmas.

Here, above all family situations—even death—is needed a sound set of values. Nor let it be said that any reference to religion is inappropriate for some. We have worked and traveled in nations over most of the globe, and have found that the Golden Rule runs like a golden thread through all of them, whether humanist, Muslim, Buddhist, Tao, Christian, or Jew.

Hearts of children may seem irreparably hurt and resentments too deep to heal, but the record of successful discipline clearly gives the edge to those who have some systematic code of ethics, usually based on belief in a divine power. If you try to make decisions with young lives without reference to a consistent system of values, you will have little or no constructive discipline at all. Yet that is exactly the state of many families today.

Settle it that corporal punishment shall never be parental vengeance. Neither do you whip or spank simply to assert your authority, nor because you are physically bigger than they. You simply face them with unpleasant consequences, even painful experiences when they insist on disobeying. And make sure that the offense is one of *deliberate* action against your orders—not because they have wet their beds or dirtied their clothes or broken a dish.

The Golden Rule—your consistent disciplinary guide—permits you to do only to your children what you, in your mature wisdom, would want them to do to you if you were in their place and they in yours. If you make an effort to understand your children and to be consistently patient yourself, corporal punishment will seldom be needed in your home.

As we put some of the last touches on this book, we did another series of broadcasts with Dr. James Dobson of *Focus on the Family*. Among several topics of mutual interest, we are discussing *self-esteem* and *self-worth*. And we are reexamining the real character of children. When they are *strong-willed*, are they really strong? Or are they *self-willed and weakly disciplined?* This all makes a great deal of difference to family health!

If you look at older dictionaries, you will find that self-esteem is a self-centered word. It had a negative meaning until the last generation or two, but was given a new interpretation by narcissistic psychologists and philosophers who centered their whole idea on the intrinsic perfection of man. You were born perfect, they said. So "I'm Okay, You're Okay" has become the ruling motto of many leaders.

But you're okay and I'm okay only if I am mostly concerned about *your* welfare and you are always working first for *mine!* This is called "altruism." It finds its foundation and highest interpretation in the Golden Rule. It says "To heaven with me" instead of narcissism's "To [someplace else] with you." The Golden Rule places your neighbor's needs at least as important as yours.

If you as a parent are loving and firm and intelligently consistent with your children, you will build wills that are as strong as their development of self-control. Their self-discipline will only be as strong as your loving firmness and the consistency of your precepts and example. Such children, reared in balance, will be heirs of self-worth—in wisdom and stature and in spirit and sociability. And whatever your religion—or absence of it—they will not be bothered about self-esteem, because they are more concerned about helping and obeying and serving you and their neighbors and their God.

Genuine self-worth is not a coat you can put on your children at will. It is a deep, inner warmth and security that must be planted early and nurtured *every* day. And it may be scary, but you are the key! Here are a few hints:

Teach great values. Integrity, dependability, compassion, forgiveness and love in dealing with others automatically build deeper, richer self-worth in them, especially when you physically do things *with* them. Make them feel needed and depended on. Read them great true character stories. Give them tapes. Teach them to appreciate good music and worthy realistic art.

Be candid. Don't pretend to be perfect. Let your children know that you realize that you make mistakes, too. I remember the look on Dennis' face one time—and his hug afterward—when I apologized for getting after him for taking the car without permission, not realizing that he had acted in an emergency to help a sick neighbor. Honesty here brings a genuine humility that all great parents exude. Such humility is not degrading. It is ennobling. You need not go into gory details of your past moral lapses or lusts. Keep those to yourself. Simply be up front in things that concern your children. Don't try to cover obvious errors. Correct them.

Be creative. Surprise them. Do special things at odd times. Tuck notes between their bed sheets or by their toothbrushes: "You did a great job on the vacuuming today" or "Your hair was beautifully combed; I'm so proud." Slip a dollar bill or a five- or ten-dollar note in a favorite textbook or Torah or Bible, with a couple of tickets to a favorite event, with your business card or a smiley drawn on an attached card or slip of paper.

Grant authority commensurate with their demonstrated ability to accept responsibility. And remind them of your plan. It may begin with picking up their own toys soon after they walk. And it will crown out when they are responsible enough to take out the family car. Authority that rewards responsibility is sweet indeed. And parents' actions speak louder than words.

▀▄▀▄▀▄ Afterword: The Stripes of Love ▀▄▀▄▀▄

During my early teens my father taught me a lesson about punishment I will never forget. It might very well be called an addendum to the previous chapter. Yet it is much more and we believe provides a fitting close for this book. In telling you this story, we remind you that there will likely be times when the only thing you can do is to switch or spank or provide other similar reminders of your wisdom and love, with the certain risk that you will be seen as brutal, unmerciful, cruel, even evil. Yet you dare not let your sympathy overcome your wisdom. Your mind must rule in firmness, consistency, and love.

Of course, if you have the patience that marks a great parent, you will never punish in anger. And you can do this best when you live a temperate life.[1] Yet there are times when punishment normally administered for a certain act will find another way, a special way, the way of wisdom, compassion, and love. Sometimes it will be with a rod—rarely, we hope; and sometimes it will be another way. . . .

As boys went in my early years, I was considered quite well behaved, but some thought it was only because I could not find enough trouble to get into. My mind raced to contrive all kinds of mischief. Pretending to be good, I was often bad. Appreciative of the beautiful, I was also curious about evil.

I was the troubled son of a widower, a boy handicapped from early age who became a stepson, filled with self-doubt by a well-intentioned missionary aunt who privately passed the word that I would never amount to anything. I had so much

211

self-doubt that I had a nightly fear that my new mother would report me to Dad—more from my conscience guilt than from a vindictive mom.

My heart was also susceptible to affection and compassion. Dad, although a strict disciplinarian, was a fountain of warmth and thoughtfulness. Such was the salve of my emotional, and sometimes physical, wounds. And therein lay my first practical lessons on parental suffering. I remember how at age six, I was playing chauffeur in the beautiful 1922 Buick Phaeton Dad had bought. And I remember releasing the emergency brake. I remember Dad's long legs stretching out amazingly fast as he raced to catch the big car when it started rolling backward down the hill. Jumping on the running board, he shoved me over and grabbed the hand brake and saved my life. But he never punished me; he didn't even say much at the moment.

But he was scared! A few years later I was caught in a challenge to my ego. My friend, Billy Wells, invited me to go bike riding. I was to use his brother John's classy vehicle. I had none of my own. Dad thought that they were dangerous in those days, for there was no such thing as a boulevard stop or traffic signal, and quite a few kids were being killed or maimed. He warned that we might "get run over." Still, how could I tell Billy that I couldn't ride with him? After all, I was bigger and even a little older than he. So I consented to ride "just around the house."

But soon Billy was zigzagging down the block, and of course I had to follow. To my surprise and certain fear, he turned out onto Montrose Avenue, our main street in that California town where in those days there was a Toonerville Trolley. I followed shakily, for I had little or no experience on bicycles. Then in an effort to avoid getting the bike wheels caught in the grooves by the streetcar tracks, I swung over into the path of a big old Chevrolet, totally unaware that anyone else was on the road. Mr. Ink pressed his loud old "O-u-gah" horn, but that only confused me more.

He ran squarely over me, mangling the bike all around me. My conscience bothered me so acutely that the only thing I could say was, "Did I hurt your car, Mister?" But Mr. Ink almost had a heart attack. He thought he had killed me and rushed me home to nurse my few scratches. Still Dad didn't even bawl me out. He knew when I had enough. He actually suffered more than I.

After a particularly daring series of escapades—in which I had escaped all punishment except my conscience—there came the inevitable time of reckoning. And Dad knew how to reckon! I had often felt his lashes from the round thong off the old treadle sewing machine or from the belt he drew gracefully and threateningly from the top of his trousers. So often, in fact, did this drama unfold that the other kids generated a sort of perpetual pity, wondering what and why and when should be next. There seldom was a question about how. Dad always had that well in hand. And I—with bared bottom—was usually the actor on center stage.

It really was about time again for me to get a licking. I had missed getting caught for starting a grass fire, which could have burned down the whole community. There were dry foxtail weeds which were commonly ignited by bright sunshine magnified through a glass bottle in the grass, so since they did not ask me, I let them think that was the cause. The fact was that I lit the fire, while playing with matches, curious as to how much it would take to get those highly inflammable weeds burning. I had no idea that a gust of wind would come up suddenly and sweep the fire across those neighboring lots toward the corner service station at Ocean View and Foothill. I was really a little liar to let them think I was innocent, but I didn't get caught, except by my conscience.

I was usually much better behaved when I was with my big brother Charles. He was a good influence. But on some occasions when either he or I would have to stay after school, I would walk the two miles home over Collins Hill alone. This was a great time to roll dry brown sagebrush blossoms into homemade cigarettes and have a smoke with all the pretensions a nine-year-old could muster. I felt very evil, but also independent. Again I never got caught, except by my conscience.

But one night I got in trouble "over nothing"—at least my conscience didn't bother me a bit. I started a quarrel with my little sister Loraine by insisting that she wasn't getting the dishes dry. I was washing them, and with beautiful self-righteousness, I saw a stray drip or two on the stacked dishes. She then proceeded to find a speck or two I had not washed off. We were on our way to framing one of those little brother-little sister dramas. About that time Dad happened to be in the other room listening, and I didn't know it. So he took me in hand. In his BIG hand.

I walked with the slow tread of a doomed man into the corner bedroom. There, perpetually decorating the inside closet wall was that round leather thong half a centimeter in diameter. It had once driven Grandma Moore's old Singer treadle machine, but now it more often drove me to tears. My little sister already had regrets and, with Charles, was in tearful anticipation for me. It might be called "pity for the black sheep."

Dad was now sitting on one of the beds that was otherwise covered by a spread which our grandmother had crocheted during many evening story hours. That thought didn't comfort me. His head was bowed in deep thought. I don't wonder now, when I think of the impossibility of his second son.

I hesitated at the doorway, my mind thrashing with exaggerated thoughts of the anguish to come. Yet even without exaggeration, that thong had a habit of leaving painful welts on my bottom and thighs.

"Come here, son," Dad beckoned quietly, looking up sort of bewildered at me, apparently very tired after a long day's work. Really I felt almost as sorry for him as I did for myself. I remember thinking how much it would relieve us both if he just did not bother this time. But Dad was too consistent for that.

Then I was startled to see him put both arms out in a gesture of tenderness and mercy. He held me for a few moments in silence. Then uttering the briefest prayer—at a time when I thought I would prefer a really long one—he released me and began unbuttoning his shirt.

"This time," he nodded soberly, "I am going to let you do it." And he handed me the miserable thong, adding in desperation, "After all, I am responsible for this home. We can't have this constant quarreling. And I don't know what else to do."

No amount of persuasion would deter him. I had to lay it on.

Charles and Loraine listened from around the corner, astonished. For them and for me that night, a new meaning came to the old saying that until now I had always considered a farce: "It hurts me worse than it does you!"

Never did Dad teach us a more effective corporal lesson. I do not recall ever having a whipping after that. Or have I forgotten them because I understood better? I have watched the Flagellantes of the Philippines, who employed others to cut their backs with paddles made of broken glass and then whip them as each carried a heavy cross along a levee to the village church. I have watched the self-inflicted suffering of pilgrims at La Scala Sancta in Rome as they climbed that long, steep stairway on their hands and knees. Yet none of these has impressed me so deeply as the father who took those stripes in my place.

▀▀▀▀▀▀▀▀▀▀▀ Study Guide ▀▀▀▀▀▀▀▀▀▀▀

Uses for This Study Guide

The helpful, practical study you are about to embark upon centers on the critical ministry of parental discipline. If you are a parent, you already know the importance of consistent discipline in your relationship with your children—whether or not you have been able to achieve consistency. If you are not yet a parent, this study will help equip you for the important ministry of parenting which lies ahead.

Whenever possible, moms and dads should be encouraged to attend these studies *together*. Parenting is a joint effort and greater family unity can be achieved when both parents are involved. This study guide has been organized into thirteen hour-long sessions in order to facilitate its use in Sunday school classes that meet for a thirteen-week quarter. But you can use this guide in many other settings, such as midweek studies and neighborhood groups. Special suggestions for retreats are included at the end of this guide.

Materials Needed

No matter how you use this guide, make sure your group members have the necessary materials to benefit from it. Each group member should obtain his or her own copy of *Home Built Discipline* and bring it to each study session, along with a Bible. He or she may also want to bring a small notebook or journal for writing down personal reflections, prayers, or Scripture verses at the end of each lesson.

Anyone Can Lead These Study Sessions

No expert teacher is required to teach this course, only group members willing to serve as discussion leaders. You may even have a different group member serve as the leader for each session. The book and the Bible itself serve as the "teachers." *Anyone who plans to serve as a leader should read the "Seven Shoulds and Should Nots for Leaders."*

Each session of the study guide includes certain features: "Getting Started" (questions and activities that get the group warmed up), "Probing the Text" (questions and readings that explore the text and the Bible), and "Applying the Truth" (questions and activities that help group members apply the lesson personally). Most sessions include the writing out of a personal reflection, application, or prayer by each group member. This is because of the simple truth that the more involved we are in our learning—not just listening, but also speaking, writing, and doing—the better we learn.

Seven Shoulds and Should Nots for Study Leaders

1. Read over the session and corresponding book chapter carefully before the meeting. This way you can anticipate topics of discussion that may be difficult or sensitive and can note materials that need to be gathered. (The leader should always make sure paper and pencils are available, for example.)

2. Avoid lecturing. Merely ask the questions from the study guide and try to stimulate discussion. At times this may mean encouraging a quiet person to contribute ideas or calling a halt to a discussion that's gone off on a tangent.

3. Remember not to act as the "expert." Group members should not expect you to judge whether or not their answers to questions are correct. No one has a printed list of right answers to this study; the group must try to judge for itself.

4. Avoid answering the questions, if at all possible, but encourage group participation instead. One veteran discussion leader recommends counting to ten before answering a question you've asked. That gives group members enough time to speak up. Silence isn't bad; it gives everyone time to think.

5. Watch the clock during the meeting. General time estimates for the parts of each session are provided in this guide, and the parts total one hour. It's important to be aware of how the time used for one part affects the time left for the others—and be willing to prod the group on to the next question.

It's especially important to save the last few minutes of the meeting for the wrap-up, when group members have a quiet time to pray, copy Scripture verses, and make personal pledges.

6. Delegate duties so that as many people as possible are involved in each session. For example, when the study guide suggests that a definition be recorded on the chalkboard or that a Scripture passage be read aloud, the leader may ask other group members to do these tasks.

7. Make sure that each session opens and closes with prayer. The group needs the Holy Spirit's help in understanding God's truth and applying it to their lives.

Session 1
"More Than Punishment"
Introduction

Before the Session

Several days before the class starts, communicate the following information by telephone, note, or church bulletin announcement to parents who will be attending this class: (1) if possible, each parent or couple should bring to the first session a family portrait—as large as possible—to decorate the room during the thirteen weeks of this class; (2) each individual should bring a notebook and pen for recording personal insights during the class; (3) each person or couple should be prepared to purchase a copy of the class text, *Home Built Discipline*, at the first session (unless the book is being provided at no cost to class members).

Getting Started (20 min.)

1. Take turns displaying your family portraits and introducing yourselves and your children (in the pictures) to each other.

2. Each individual or couple briefly share one of your most hilarious moments as a parent (for example, a water fight with your children or your child's attempt to dress up in your clothes). After everyone has commented, briefly share another parenting experience which was either frustrating, trying, or frightening (for example, a child lost in a shopping center or a child breaking one of your crystal goblets).

3. Distribute copies of *Home Built Discipline* and turn to the poem "Enjoy Those Wet Oatmeal Kisses While You Can" on pages 9-10. The poem reminds parents of the importance of cherishing their children through the sometimes frustrating, trying, and frightening years of their training and disciplining. Take turns reading aloud the short paragraphs until you have read the entire poem.

Probing the Text (30 min.)

4. Write the word "Discipline" on the chalkboard or a large sheet of newsprint for all to see. Brainstorm several synonyms or definitions for discipline and write them down as they are given.

5. Many parents equate discipline with punishment. This concept may show up in some of the definitions which are given. But the authors stress that discipline involves much more than punishment. Read aloud the paragraph at the bottom of page 24 which begins, "Discipline is much broader than punishment."

The authors say, "Discipline is an automobile; punishment is the brakes." Can you think of other descriptive contrasts for discipline and punishment based on this paragraph? Share them.

6. Take turns reading aloud the first three paragraphs under the heading "Prevention Rather Than Remedy" on page 17. Then discuss the following questions:

What key words for understanding proper discipline do you see in these paragraphs? Write them for all to see as they are given.

Why do you think some parents forgo preventive discipline with their children and resort only to remedy and punishment?

What are the negative results for parents and children when proper discipline is shunned?

What percentage of your discipline plan would you say is preventive? remedial?

7. The Bible provides some helpful guidelines for parents on the subject of discipline. Read aloud Deuteronomy 6:1-7 from at least two different translations.

What is the ultimate goal of discipline in the Christian home?

What benefits are promised to families who follow God's plan for discipline?

Who is the most positive model of parental discipline you know (that is, someone who is a living example of the parent in this passage)?

Applying the Truth (10 min.)

8. Complete one or both of the following statements in writing in your notebook:

My greatest personal need as a disciplining parent at this time in my life is . . .

My primary personal hope for this study on discipline is . . .

9. Share your completed statement(s) with at least one other person. Pray for each other and for the sessions ahead, asking God to fulfill the needs and hopes you have identified.

Assignment
Read Chapters 1 and 2 in *Home Built Discipline*.

Session 2

"A Pattern to Follow"
Chapters 1 and 2

Getting Started (10 min.)

1. Using a felt marker, draw the outline of a child, life-sized if possible, on a large sheet of butcher paper. Write above the outline, "The Perfect Child." Take turns writing on the outline specific descriptions of the perfect child. For example, someone may write near the ears, "Always washes behind his ears." Someone may write over the area of the heart, "Memorizes all his Sunday school verses." Write as many descriptions of the perfect child as possible in five minutes. Enjoy this exercise in group fantasizing!

2. There are no perfect children, of course, just as there are no perfect parents. However, parents do have the opportunity to shape their children for the better through discipline.

Read aloud the last half of the paragraph at the bottom of page 25, beginning with the words "You mold young lives just as the master sculptor shapes his clay." This is an inspiring description of the parent's role. But sometimes parents see themselves more as repair persons, picking up the broken pieces of their children's lives and gluing them back together.

What percentage of the time do you perceive yourself as a sculptor and what percentage of the time do you perceive yourself as a repair person?

Probing the Text (40 min.)

3. On pages 23 and 24, author Raymond Moore shares that he learned discipline as a child by being a disciple of his brother Charles and his father. The authors suggest that discipling is a significant part of the process of parental discipline.

Take turns completing the following statements: "A disciple is someone who . . ."; "A discipler is someone who . . ." List the key characteristics of each for all to see.

4. Read Matthew 4:18-22 aloud.

What were the major characteristics of Jesus' relationship with His disciples?

Do some or all of these characteristics apply to parents who are discipling their children? Why or why not?

Which of these characteristics do you identify in yourself as a discipler of your children?

Which characteristics need further development?

5. The Moores go on to explain that discipling children involves at least three elements: example, training, and education. Read Ephesians 6:4 aloud from at least two different translations.

Are these three elements of discipleship present in this verse? If so, how?

6. Discuss the following questions about the qualities of example, training, and education in the discipling of children:

What are the most important areas in which a parent must serve as an example (see pp. 23-24)?

What is the difference between training and education (see pp. 26-27)? Why is each important in its own right?

In which areas of discipline—example, training, or education—do you think most Christian parents do the best job? the worst job?

Why do parents tend to do a better job in some areas than in others?

7. The Moores stress that disciplining children requires rewarding them with authority only in areas where they show responsibility. Read Luke 10:1-20 aloud.

What authority did Jesus grant to the seventy-two?

What responsibilities did He expect them to fulfill?

From your recollection of Christ's ministry, how had He prepared His disciples for their assignment through example, training, and education?

8. Work together to write a concise job description for a parent as a discipler of children based on today's discussion. Write the job description in your notebook as a reminder and prayer request.

Applying the Truth (10 min.)

9. On a scale of one to ten, ten being high, how would you rate yourself as a discipler of your children in each of the following areas: example, training, education? Write a number rating for each in your notebook, then share them briefly with at least one other person.

10. How would you rate yourself on the skill of giving authority to your children only where they have fulfilled responsibility? Write a number rating from one to ten in your notebook, then share it with someone.

11. Use your ratings as a focal point for group prayer. Ask God to sculpt you into discipling parents.

Assignment

Read Chapter 3 in *Home Built Discipline*.

Session 3

"A Creative Approach"
Chapter 3

Getting Started (5 min.)

1. There is no other child in the world just like your child. He or she is unique and in need of a creative approach to discipline based on his or her unique characteristics and abilities.

Each individual or couple briefly respond to the following question: How are your children different from most other children? You may comment about physical characteristics ("He's taller than most other kids in his class"), social characteristics ("She is the organizer and manager when she plays with her friends"), spiritual characteristics ("He has already memorized the books of the Bible"), or any other feature which sets your child apart.

Probing the Text (45 min.)

2. In Chapter 3 the Moores suggest that developing a unique, creative approach for disciplining your child can be helped by examining some popular classroom approaches.

How can an understanding of classroom discipline techniques help parents form their own creative plan?

Are you aware of the classroom discipline techniques employed in the schools your children attend? If so, what are they?

3. Discuss the following questions to help you review the highlights of the three approaches to classroom discipline discussed in this chapter (Lee Canter's Assertive Discipline, Rudolf Dreikur's Logical Consequences, and Thomas Gordon's Teacher Effectiveness Training, pp. 33-37):

What are the strengths of each approach?

What are the weaknesses of each approach?

4. Read aloud the parable of the lost son from Luke 15:11-31.

Which of the three classroom approaches most closely parallels the way the father in this parable disciplined his younger son? his older son?

How might the story have been changed if the father had used either of the other two approaches?

5. Read aloud the first paragraph under the heading "Selecting the Best from Authorities (The Moore Approach)" at the bottom of page 47.

Do you think the lost son's father followed this advice? If so, how and to what extent? If not, how did he fail to follow it?

6. The Moores state, "Ultimately you will develop your own system of discipline. You will have your own style. As any skilled potter forms the clay into a graceful vessel, you will study your 'material' and bring out noble creations" (p. 47). Then they go on to suggest six "hints" for developing your own creative approach (see pp. 48-49).

Review the first five hints together (the sixth suggests a number of general, minor tips) and reduce each one to a key phrase of five words or less. Write these phrases for all to see.

7. Divide into five groups of equal size. Assign each group one of the first five hints for creative, pro-active discipline presented on pages 48 and 49.

Imagine that the younger son in the parable has approached his parents to tell them he wants to take his inheritance and leave. How would the parents respond if they followed each of the five hints? Discuss the question in your small group as it applies to your assigned hint. Then appoint two of your members to role-play a conversation between the father and mother as they discuss how following this hint either helped or hindered the son in this situation. Take 1-2 minutes for each group.

8. Would the story of the lost son have been different if his parents had followed the five hints in this chapter? If so, how? If not, why not?

If you had been the parent in the parable, how would you have responded to the situation?

Applying the Truth (10 min.)
9. Review the five brief statements summarizing the hints for creative discipline from this session. Identify one hint you are successfully implementing at this time. Write it in your notebook and cite an example of your success.

10. Which hint are you having the greatest difficulty implementing in your discipline plan? Write it in your notebook and cite an example.

Begin your prayer time by thanking God for the successes you are experiencing. Then lift to Him those areas of frustration you noted, asking His guidance in developing your creative discipline plan.

Assignment
Read Chapters 4 and 5 in *Home Built Discipline*.

Session 4

"Parental Control Develops Self-Control"
Chapters 4 and 5

Getting Started (10 min.)

1. Bring several recent newspapers to class and distribute them among class members. Scan the pages for articles reporting children or youth who have become involved in bad situations (such as gang activity, drugs, or rebellion). For each article you find, try to determine if the parents are identified as being directly involved or responsible for the child's problem. What are the parents' responses to their children's problems, if mentioned? Share your findings with each other.

Probing the Text (40 min.)

2. In this section of *Home Built Discipline,* the authors stress that attempts to discipline small children by reasoning with them usually end in failure because "at age three or four children are not able to reason consistently enough to fully understand such explanations" (p. 53). The Moores go on to state, "If you assume that your children will grasp the logic of your instructions and your actions before they have developed enough to be able to reason consistently, you may burn out" (p. 56). What kinds of burnout do you think they are referring to?

3. The authors use the case study of eighteen-month-old David in Chapter 5 to illustrate the importance of controlling a young child's behavior "at least in the first few years before he is able to reason" (p. 59). Dorothy Moore underscores the importance of control by warning Mrs. Doran, "If he does not submit to your will, he will not be able to submit to any authority, including God's" (p. 59).

Read 2 Kings 2:21-25 and Proverbs 19:18 aloud.

Why should we consider discipline a life-and-death matter?

Other than physical death, in what ways can lack of discipline contribute to a child's "death" (for example, emotional death, relational death, etc.)?

Do you know any families in which the lack of discipline is "killing" the child in some way? In what ways is the parents' neglect negatively affecting the child(ren)?

4. Dorothy's response to Mrs. Doran suggests several ways for her to establish control in her relationship with David. Read aloud the paragraph at the top of page 60 which begins, "In general you should calmly say what you mean. . . ."

What are the key words in this paragraph which summarize Dorothy's general approach to control?

5. Read Galatians 6:7-10 aloud.

How many parallels can you think of between the tasks of tending a garden and tending a child with firm, loving discipline? between the results of consistent gardening techniques and consistent discipline with a child?

6. The Moores suggest throughout their book that early, consistent parental control leads to effective self-control in a child. Read 1 Peter 1:13-16.

What benefits are suggested in these verses for the Christian who reaches adulthood having learned self-control through parental control?

7. Review Mrs. Moore's eleven suggestions to Mrs. Doran on pages 60-64, as summarized below. Select four or five which are especially appropriate for the parents in your class.

For each one you select, ask: How will following this suggestion contribute to the development of a child's self-control? What negative behaviors or circumstances may result in a child or parent if this suggestion is ignored?

1. Control through routine.
2. Never give in to a tantrum.
3. Encourage good behavior.
4. Spank when appropriate.
5. Don't reward crying or whining.
6. Reward good behavior.
7. Involve the father in the child's life.
8. Direct interests outwardly.
9. Outline expectations and consequences.
10. Remove all hope for the forbidden.
11. Pray for yourself and your child.

Applying the Truth (10 min.)

8. Select one or two of the suggestions discussed today which you need to implement in order for you and your child to reap the benefits of parental control and self-control. In your notebook, write a brief letter to your child explaining your commitment to develop his self-control through consistent parental control. This letter is not for your child to read or hear; it is for your benefit, helping you verbalize the importance of exercising parental control.

9. Form groups of three or four and read your letters to one another. Pray together that God will help you equip your children with self-control through your commitment to parental control.

Assignment
Read Chapters 6 through 8 in *Home Built Discipline*.

Session 5

"What Makes Your Child Tick?"
Chapters 6 through 8

Getting Started (5-10 min.)

1. Most Christian parents discipline their children without really understanding their developmental characteristics and needs. Do you strongly agree? moderately agree? moderately disagree? strongly disagree?

Designate a different area of the room (wall, corner, etc.) for each of the four responses. Go stand in the area which represents your response, and then allow one or two volunteers from each area to defend each position.

This is an opinion issue, not a right-or-wrong one. Enjoy lively discussion and debate, but allow room for differences of opinion.

Probing the Text (40-45 min.)

2. The authors of *Home Built Discipline* say, "Nearly all discipline problems in one way or another originate from a lack of understanding of the way children 'tick' . . . some knowledge of children's development trends can make life much easier for both you and them" (p. 56).

What are some ways parents can gain insight into their child's developmental stages?

What are some ways Christian parents can help each other in this task?

3. Read aloud the paragraph in the middle of page 67 which begins, "Given time, babies' instincts combine with intellectual growth . . . ." Review the important guidelines for disciplining children in their first five years by calling out key words and phrases from chapter 6 (for example, control, routine, order, curiosity, physical growth). Write these topics for all to see.

4. Read Proverbs 22:6 aloud in at least two different translations.

What is the parent's primary training role for each of the topics you have listed from Chapter 6?

5. Read aloud the first paragraph of Chapter 7 on page 90. The Moores go on to state that a child's transition years—age six to eight—are "a period when they should be getting their physical and emo-

tional act together before formal schooling, sometime after age eight" (p. 91).

Do you agree that home schooling is preferable to institutional schooling for most children under age eight?

What is good about home schooling for these children?

What circumstances may make institutional schooling "absolutely necessary"?

6. As children move into adolescence, peer involvement tends to dilute parental influence and control. The authors state, "Peer relationships are important to them, but they will be independent thinkers if their elective time has been more with you than with their friends and if your times and counsel are easily available for their needs" (p. 101).

What are some ways Christian parents can encourage their preteens and teenagers to spend a significant amount of their "elective time" with them without discouraging important peer relationships?

7. Read aloud Luke 2:41-52.

What words or phrases suggest to you that Jesus was becoming an independent thinker at age twelve?

What suggests to you that Jesus' parents did not discourage healthy peer relationships?

Applying the Truth (10 min.)

8. Write the names and ages of each of your children on a blank sheet in your notebook. Beside each name write a brief memo reminding yourself of an insight about each child's development from today's discussion that you need to apply to your training of them.

Examples:
Amy, age four: Establish a more consistent mealtime and bedtime schedule.

Brett, age six: Investigate the possibilities of home schooling him for at least two years (curriculum, state requirements, etc.).*

Clint, age eleven: Schedule one or two afternoons a week for a special activity together (snack after school, bike ride, profit-making project, neighborhood service, etc.).

9. Reread Luke 2:52. Center your prayer time on being God's instrument of training and discipline to help your child develop mentally, physically, spiritually, and socially.

---

*For more information on readiness for school or home schooling, send a self-addressed, stamped envelope to Box 1, Camas, WA 98607. Also for further reading on the subject, you can read the Moores' books *Better Late than Early*, *Home Grown Kids*, or *Home School Burnout*.

Assignment
Read Chapters 9 and 10 in *Home Built Discipline*.

Session 6
"Example and Order"
Chapters 9 and 10

Getting Started (10-15 min.)

1. On a blank sheet of paper draw or doodle something which represents a positive behavior you learned from a parent's example. For example, you may draw a dollar sign because you observed your father sit down to write checks and pay bills promptly every payday, a practice you now follow. Or you may draw a steeple representing your parents' faithfulness in getting you to church every Sunday, which is now your commitment to your family.

2. Then draw or doodle something which represents a positive family tradition from your childhood. For example, you may draw a plate stacked high with pancakes representing your family's traditional Saturday morning breakfast. Or you may draw something which represents the way your family celebrated birthdays or which reminds you of your bedtime ritual.

   Share your doodles with at least one other person sitting nearby.

Probing the Text (40 min.)

3. The first building block of commonsense discipline is warm responsiveness and example. The authors state, "Parent and teacher response, along with example, is a most powerful educational tool and is one of the best guarantors of sound discipline" (p. 110).

   Read Matthew 5:14-16 aloud. Divide into groups of three or four persons. Work together in your groups to paraphrase this passage so that its message on example is directly applied to parents. For example, your paraphrase may begin, "Dad and Mom, you are shining examples in the world of your home." Make sure someone in your group writes down your paraphrase.

   After a few minutes of small group discussion, share your paraphrases with the other groups.

4. The Moores suggest, "Getting your own life in order as a parent is the first step in rearing well-behaved children" (p. 106). Brainstorm some key areas in which Christian parents must get their lives in order as positive examples (such as personal organization and schedule). List them for all to see.

From the list you developed, which are the top two or three areas you think Christian parents especially need to attend to?

Which are your top two or three areas of need?

5. The authors contend that depriving our children of parental attention and response is robbery, and that institutionalizing them *unnecessarily* in day-care facilities and preschools is child abuse (p. 108). Do you agree with these strong claims? Why or why not? If circumstances *require* both parents to work, what alternatives may be better than institutional care?

In what ways can parents who must institutionalize their children for some reason compensate for reduced attention and response?

6. Return to small groups. Read Ephesians 5:29-32 aloud. Half of the groups develop a list of do's for parents, from this passage, with regard to their need be responsive to their children. The other half of the groups develop a list of don'ts for parents from the same passage.

After a few minutes of small group discussion, share your lists of do's and don'ts with the other groups.

7. The second building block of commonsense discipline is routine, regularity, and order. The authors state, "Nearly all children up through the early teens find security in regularity at home" (p. 112).

Why do you think attention to schedule, neatness, and predictability so positively affects the security factor in children?

Why do you think secure children respond better to discipline?

8. How do the following sometimes complicate our efforts to provide routine, regularity, and order for our families: television, school activities, church activities, your children's friends, relatives?

Can you think of other obstacles which interfere with routine, regularity, and order in your home?

9. How can Christian parents overcome these complications and obstacles without isolating their children from the positive contributions of television, school activities, church activities, friends, relatives, etc.?

How do you balance these influences in your home?

Applying the Truth (5-10 min.)

10. Complete the following statements in writing in your notebook:

The key thought for me to remember and apply from this session about being an example is . . .

The key thought for me to remember and apply about showing warm responsiveness to my children is . . .

The key thought for me to remember and apply about establishing routine, regularity, and order for my children is . . .

11. Select one of the key thoughts you have identified and share it as a prayer request with your small group from this session. Take turns praying for one another's requests.

Assignment
Read Chapters 11 and 12 in *Home Built Discipline*.

Session 7

"Working, Playing, and Serving Together"
Chapters 11 and 12

Getting Started (5 min.)
1. Take turns pantomiming your answer to one of the following questions so the other members of the class can guess it:
  What was your first money-making job as a child?
  What was your favorite pastime as a child?

Probing the Text (40 min.)
2. The third building block for commonsense discipline is constructive work and play. The Moores say: "Work is a crucially important activity for the highest form of discipline, both preventive and remedial" (p. 119). About play they write, "Give your children a chance to develop concentration and coordination as well as creativity in play, and you will discover a new spirit in them" (pp. 121-122).

  Our society tends to glamorize play, leisure, and retirement and demean work and the work ethic. Why? How should they be balanced?

  How were work and play regarded in your home as a child? Was one unduly exalted over the other?

3. Divide into several small groups and assign at least one of the following verses to each group: Proverbs 10:4; Proverbs 13:4; Proverbs 14:23; Proverbs 22:29; Ecclesiastes 9:10; Ephesians 4:28. Read your assigned verse(s) as a small group and discuss:
  What benefits do children receive when they learn good work habits?
  How do these habits and benefits assist in discipline?

4. On pages 120 and 121 the authors discuss the value of parents' involving their children in free enterprise work projects.
  What pros and cons should a family discuss before embarking on such a project?
  What responsibilities will fall to the parent who commits to such an endeavor with his children?

If you were to help your child enter into "business," what kind of business would it be? Why?

5. The Moores encourage parents to guide but not interfere in their child's business ventures.

When does parental guidance become parental interference?

How difficult would it be for you to guide your child in a work activity without interfering?

6. The Moores say, "Children are over-toyed, over-entertained, and over-amused at home, at school, and wherever they go" (p. 121). Do you agree?

What evidences of this statement do you see in the homes of other parents you know? in your own home? in your child's school?

7. What percentage of the sports and games children play today are rivalry- or competition-based? Brainstorm a list of non-competitive activities Christian parents could encourage their children toward. Then brainstorm a list of play activities parents and children can participate in together without prompting harmful rivalry or competition. Can you share an activity from your family's experience?

8. The fourth building block for commonsense discipline is service to others. The authors write, "We have easily within our reach a jewel of great price for both prevention and remedy of dependency and delinquency! The jewel is the spirit of service—to the community, state, nation, and world; to poor, needy, ill, aged, and imprisoned; to neighbors and friends and, occasionally, to someone who has done us wrong" (p. 125).

Read Galatians 5:13-14 aloud. Loving service to others is at the heart of the Christian life.

If your children looked to you as an example of service to others, what kind of example would they find: sterling, pretty good, plain ol' vanilla, in need of repair, or "help!" (choose one)?

In what areas can your example of service stand significant improvement?

9. According to Chapter 12, what positive qualities result in a child who is involved in the selfless service of others (for example, self-worth)?

Are these qualities helpful in facilitating parental discipline? Why or why not?

Applying the Truth (15 min.)

10. Discuss as a class a service project you could complete together with your children:

Examples:
> Visit a convalescent home and take flowers to the patients.
> Volunteer to clean the church's vehicles (church bus, vans, pastor's car) inside and out.
> Perform a secret S.O.S. mission for an elderly family in the church (see p. 126).

Once you have decided on a project, set a prospective date and assign responsibilities for preparation.

11. On a smaller scale, jot down plans in your notebook for getting involved with your own children this week in each of the following: a work project; a non-competitive play activity; a service project to a neighbor, shut-in, etc.

Close by praying for each other.

Assignment
Read Chapters 13 and 14 in *Home Built Discipline*.

Session 8

"Involvement and Consistency"
Chapters 13 and 14

Getting Started (5-10 min.)
1. Aside from normal daily activities, what does your family purposely do together (family night once a week, scouting, 4-H, summer vacations)?

On a scale of one to ten, with ten being high, how would you rate the success of these activities in complementing parental discipline?

Probing the Text (40 min.)
2. The fifth building block of commonsense discipline is involvement with your children through camaraderie, courtesy, and communication. The Moores state, "No matter what the projects may be, make it your high priority to be involved. Too many parents allow other people or institutions, though well-meaning and often efficient, to do their parenting for them" (p. 129).

Jesus was not a parent, but He did model the kind of loving involvement with His twelve disciples—especially the inner circle of Peter, James, and John—that parents should practice with their children. Read aloud Matthew 4:18-22.

How did Jesus display His willingness to become involved with Peter, James, and John in their activities?

Can you think of other occasions when Jesus involved Himself in the lives and activities of those He came to serve?

In which of your child's current activities are you actively involved? In which could you become involved if you decided to commit yourself to do so?

3. Read aloud Matthew 26:36-46.

How did Jesus display His willingness to involve His disciples in His activities?

Can you think of other occasions when He called His followers to get involved in something He was doing?

In which of your activities have you involved your children (taken them to work with you, included them in a service club activity, involved them in household chores)?

In which of your activities could you include them if you decided to commit yourself to do so?

4. The Moores encourage parents to involve themselves with their children through listening: "Adults are considered sources of information, but children also need to express their feelings, fears, ideas, and attitudes to them. . . . Listening will give you a running start in your discipline" (p. 129). The authors relate the story of a young boy whose father ignored his excited pleas to come watch their luggage as it was being loaded onto a plane.

What seemingly important interests sometimes keep you from listening to your children in similar situations?

What must you do to assure greater attentiveness to what your children have to say?

5. Patience is an important element in listening. The authors comment, "Wait your children out, no matter how silly, boring, or unnecessary their talk may seem" (p. 131). Read Matthew 19:13-14 aloud. In the midst of Jesus' crowded life, children were important to Him.

Is your busy life a cause of your impatience with your children? If so, what must happen to your schedule in order to increase your patience?

6. The sixth building block of commonsense discipline is consistency and unity. The Moores admonish: "Set your goals carefully, plan your work, and work your plan. Do your best never to give a command and then forget it or fail to follow through; this is the sure road to defeat in family or school or any discipline anywhere" (pp. 134-135).

What specific implications for consistency do you think apply to a parent's personal life? to a parent's guidelines for a child's discipline?

7. The Moore's son Dennis proposes that parents establish a consistent "tentative tolerance threshold" (TTT). Read aloud the two para-

graphs on page 135 which describe TTT, beginning with, "As one method toward your goal of consistency . . . ."

What is your current TTT, if you have one?

What TTT would you like to establish and stick by for disciplining your children?

8. The Moores stress that "your TTT should be established in counsel with your spouse so that there is unity in consistency" (p. 136).

What obstacles must a father and mother overcome in order to present a unified front before their children?

What sacrifices must parents make to insure the unity and consistency of their discipline?

Applying the Truth (10-15 min.)

9. The following questions will guide you to some practical applications of today's topics with your children. Write the answers in your notebook. If possible, write in the dates (preferably within the next two weeks) when you can get involved with your children in these ways:

Which of your children's activities will you involve yourself in (e.g., attend their classes at school, help them with one of their chores, etc.)?

Which of your activities will you involve your children in (e.g., take them to work with you one day, include them as you complete one of your chores or errands, etc.)?

Write three questions you will ask your children during your time together so you can practice your listening skills (e.g., What is the happiest part of your day? If you could plan a vacation for our family, where would it be and what would we do?).

10. Join in prayer with other parents for the success of your endeavors toward involvement and consistency.

Assignment

Read Chapters 15 and 16 in *Home Built Discipline*.

Session 9

"Prompting Thought and Giving Encouragement" Chapters 15 and 16

Getting Started (10 min.)

1. Complete the following statements:

The person in my life who has stimulated my thinking the most was/is . . .

He/she stimulated me by . . .

The person in my life who has been the greatest encouragement to me was/is . . .

He/she encouraged me by . . .

Share your responses with at least one other person.

Probing the Text (40 min.)

2. The seventh building block for commonsense discipline is helping children learn how to think for themselves. The authors believe that "learning to be thinkers rather than mere reflectors of others' thoughts should be a constant goal in the education of your children" (p. 139).

How do parents tend to short-circuit the necessary process of a child's learning to think for himself?

In what ways does a parent allow the child's environment (school, television) to do his thinking for him?

3. Review the Moores' three-step "recipe" for transforming our children into thinkers (pp. 139-140). Form some guidelines for balancing truthful responsiveness and humor.

When is it okay to use humor?

When is it not okay?

The Moores caution that deep thinking is generally beyond the ability of children under eight years old, but they encourage parents to stimulate them with *why* and *how* questions as early as age three.

What kinds of questions can you ask to stimulate your child's thinking about God? about healthy family relationships? about the importance of routine, regularity, and order in their lives? about obedience?

4. The Moores contend that forcing our children into institutional care before they are able to reason consistently (age eight or older) detracts from their development as thinkers.

How can parents who find it necessary (or elect) to place their children in day-care or public school encourage creative, individual thinking?

What kinds of *why* or *how* questions would be appropriate in this setting?

5. In Chapter 15 the Moores relate the findings of McCurdy on the topic of genius: "Your children need (1) a great deal of *you*, (2) very little of their agemates, and (3) a rich experience in exploring for themselves" (p. 141).

Although your goal is to produce thinkers, not necessarily geniuses, do you think that McCurdy's formula is a good recommendation for discipline?

Why or why not?

What would it take for you to implement his formula in your present family structure?

6. The eighth building block of commonsense discipline is encouragement and appreciation as displayed through speech and touch. The Moores say, "If you are consistent and warm in your displays of gratitude and affection, they will understand when you have to restrict or punish them" (p. 143).

Solomon wrote a number of proverbs about the importance of positive speech in relationships. Sometimes we forget to apply these to the most intimate of relationships: the family. Read aloud the following verses from Proverbs: 12:18; 15:1; 15:23; 16:24. As you read each verse, paraphrase it so that it specifically challenges parents regarding their communication with their children. For example, Proverbs 12:18 may be paraphrased, "Remember, Dad and Mom: When you speak thoughtlessly to your kids, you will wound them; but your wise words of encouragement and appreciation will bring them inner health."

7. Loving pats and hugs convey volumes of encouragement and appreciation. Was physical affection openly given and received in your home as a child? If not, it may not come as easily for you now as for others whose families were affectionate.

How difficult is it for you to express affection openly to your children?

Do you sometimes resist displaying appreciation, encouragement, and affection outwardly because you don't feel these qualities inside? The Moores remind us: "Speaking and showing affection without 'feeling' warm and loving will help create the feeling" (p. 143).

8. The authors encourage parents to recognize their children's differences and compliment them accordingly: "Your goal will be to never try to make them alike except in those character and personality qualities that all good people should have," endeavoring to "maximize their strengths and minimize their weaknesses" (p. 144).

What are the particular strengths and talents you should be encouraging and appreciating in each of your children?

What are the positive character qualities which you see emerging in them?

Applying the Truth (10 min.)

9. On a sheet of notebook paper or a card, write a note of appreciation to each of your children. Encourage them by complimenting them on their strengths and achievements. Make sure your notes are warm, uplifting, and honest. Avoid flattery and syrupy platitudes. Deliver the notes in the coming week by mailing them, placing them under your children's pillows, taping them to their mirrors, etc.

10. Pray together for creative ways to encourage your children and to challenge your children to think for themselves.

Assignment
Read Chapters 17 and 18 in *Home Built Discipline.*

Session 10

"Health and Money"
Chapters 17-18

Getting Started (10 min.)
1. Letter the words *health* and *money* down the left side of a large sheet of paper on the wall.

How many stock phrases can you think of, beginning with the letters h-e-a-l-t-h, which parents use to teach or chide their children about health? For example, someone may suggest "Eat your vegetables" for *e*. Write the phrases on the sheet as they are mentioned. Try to get at least one phrase for each letter.

Do the same thing for phrases about teaching the use of money, using the letters m-o-n-e-y.

Probing the Text (40 min.)
2. The ninth building block for commonsense discipline is caring for a child's health by monitoring his diet, dress, sleep, and exercise.* The authors state: "[The] lack of information or commonsense in practice [in these areas] directly obstructs sound discipline" (p. 148). They compare the child ignored in these areas to a car which is ill-treated and which runs poorly because of it.

Without laying blame on your parents, how well did you "run" as a child?

How did attention to your health as a child affect how you responded to discipline?

3. Read Exodus 15:26, Proverbs 4:20-22, and 3 John 2 aloud.

What parallels do you see between these verses and the Moores' insistence that a child's health and productive lifestyle are interrelated?

How do these verses contrast the Moores' prescription for discipline in the home?

4. The Moores say, "What you and your children eat bears directly on

---

*For practical information on family health, you can read the Moores' book *Home Made Health*, or send a self-addressed, stamped envelope to Box 1, Camas, WA 98607.

the nature and number of discipline problems you will have around your home" (p. 149). The Moores remind us that "tastes and eating habits are developed, not inherited" (p. 151).

Why is it so difficult for a family to eat the right kinds and quantities of food?

What benefits will a child receive from having his diet and eating schedule controlled by his parents?

What is the greatest obstacle you must overcome in order to provide your child with these benefits?

5. What is the difference between the psychological and the physiological importance of guiding children to be appropriately dressed?

How well do you follow these guidelines regarding your own apparel?

Do you think your behavior in this area is affecting your children's behavior? If so, how?

6. On pages 154-156 the authors offer several practical ideas for ensuring more efficient sleep for your children. Review them briefly, then determine by concensus the tip which is most difficult for your group of parents to follow.

Why do you think this area is such a common problem?

How are you as a parent doing in this area?

7. Efficient sleep and exercise habits are as important for adults as for children in the activity of discipline.

To what extent do you agree or disagree with this statement?

What personal experiences influence how you feel about this statement?

8. The tenth building block for commonsense discipline is teaching children how to manage money. Read Matthew 6:24 aloud. (Note: The word *mammon* in many older translations of this verse is appropriately translated *money* in newer, more reliable translations.)

What does this verse communicate about the importance of teaching children how to manage money?

9. Read aloud the two paragraphs which begin at the top of page 159. Notice the statement: "Your children do not have any right to the money which *you* earn."

Would you say this statement is very harsh, harsh, about right, mild, or very mild compared to the way you have been operating in your family?

Why do you think some parents keep their children monetarily dependent on them?

10. On the topic of allowances for children, the Moores urge: "Don't

make money too easy to get. They need to work for it" (p. 160).

When is it appropriate to give money to children without having them work for it?

When should they work for the money they receive?

In what ways can Christian parents teach the priority of giving money and resources over receiving them in a culture that has those priorities reversed?

Applying the Truth (10 min.)

11. Plan the "ideal day" in the life of a family based on the guidelines for health discussed in this session. Write in your notebook a twenty-four-hour schedule which includes healthy amounts of food, rest, and exercise for both parent and child. For example, decide the best time for the family to eat, sleep, take naps, play, study, and so on. Also decide what kind of foods should be served and include some suggestions for exercise. Then compare your "ideal day" with the schedule of one other person.

12. No family lives at the level of your ideal schedule. But ideals are healthy goals toward which you can grow.

What is the first step you need to take to help your family grow toward the ideals you have listed? Write your growth step in your notebook. Then pray with a few other people, asking God to help you start growing in the right direction step by step.

Assignment

Read Chapters 19 through 21 in *Home Built Discipline*.

Session 11

Dealing with Putdowns and Down Times
Chapters 19 through 21

Getting Started (10 min.)

1. Children are a lot like balloons. They can be easily inflated with joy and even more quickly popped or deflated by disappointment or discouragement. With this in mind, share your answers to the following questions with each other:

In what ways are parents guilty of popping their child's balloon?

Why is it important to effective discipline that parents inflate their children instead of deflate them?

Probing the Text (40 min.)

2. In Chapters 19 and 20 the authors discuss the negative effects of parental putdowns and teasing on discipline. "Without intending to demean their children," the Moores explain, "parents often leave them with scars that linger a lifetime and sometimes evoke despair. This is one of the most certain and easiest ways to create your own discipline problems" (p. 164).

Why do you think putdowns and negative teasing have such a harmful effect on discipline?

3. The Moores identify several forms of putdowns which can damage a child even when your negative words and actions are unintentional: ridicule, faultfinding, comparisons, judging, name-calling, the silent treatment, etc.

Have you noticed a problem with discipline in your home which might be traced to one or more of these behaviors on your part?

If so, how do the "cause and effect" appear to be connected?

The Moores insist, "In order to build family loyalty, putdowns . . . should be forbidden, and you must set the example" (p. 164).

To what extent is the example of your relationship with other adults helping or hindering your efforts at disciplining your children?

4. Read Romans 14:19 and 1 Thessalonians 5:11 aloud. The instructions to edify—or build up—one another are vital for the Christian home.

What are some specific ways parents can obey these instructions in what they say to their children?

The Moores repeatedly mention that thoughtlessness is a main culprit leading to words which put down instead of build up. What are some practical ways parents can remind themselves to be thoughtful in what they say to their children?

5. The Moores say that placing children in school before they are ready is "one of the most pervasively practiced putdowns of all," inviting disciplinary problems such as "anxiety, frustration, failure, peer dependency, delinquency, and a low quality of socialization" (p. 168).

In what ways can home schooling combat these negative characteristics in children?

How can parents who must institutionalize their children compensate for the potentially negative impact of institutionalization?

6. The Moores say, "Humor should be cultivated and encouraged as much as teasing should be discouraged" (p. 173).

What's the difference between hurtful teasing and good-natured humor?

When is teasing okay and humor bad in relating to children?

7. Matthew 7:12 is commonly called the Golden Rule, and the Moores refer to it often as a guideline for avoiding putdowns and encouraging edification. Read it aloud from at least two translations. Then work together to paraphrase the verse so that it specifically applies to verbal putdowns and edification with children.

8. In Chapter 21 the Moores focus on discouragement and depression—down times for children—and their symptoms and causes. Review the seven symptoms presented in the chapter: hyperactivity, withdrawal, sluggishness and indifference, stubbornness and impatience, imagined needs, hostile or rebellious behavior, and psychosis.

What are the most common causes for these behaviors?

What are the most common cures suggested by the Moores for combatting these behaviors?

9. The Moores cite the importance of spiritual and moral values in releasing children from the dungeon of discouragement and depression. Read Jeremiah 15:16 and Colossians 3:15-16.

What is a primary element in God's prescription, as suggested in these verses, for replacing down times with joy and peace?

How are you ensuring that this element is present in your children's lives?

Share ideas together for positively integrating God's Word in the daily relationship between parents and children.

Applying the Truth (10 min.)

10. Write a brief memo in your notebook reminding yourself of two specific steps you can take to combat putdowns and down times in your relationship with your children. First, identify one of the practical ways for edifying your children, discussed in step 4 above, that you especially need to put into practice. Second, identify one of the ideas for sharing God's Word with your children, discussed in step 9 above, which you need to implement at home.

11. Share at least one of your written memos with a small group from the class. Pray together for wisdom and impetus from God to follow through with these positive tasks.

Assignment

Read Chapters 22 through 24 in *Home Built Discipline.*

Session 12

"Special Children and Boy/Girl Roles"
Chapters 22 through 24

Getting Started (10–15 min.)

1. In order to determine how many class members come from and/or are presently involved in nontraditional, non-"Leave-It-to-Beaver" families, raise your hand if:

• you have a stepparent(s) in addition to, or in place of, your natural parent(s)

• you and/or your spouse are stepparents to one or more of your children

• you were adopted by one or both parents

• you have any adopted children

• you were in foster care at any time during childhood

• you have ever had foster children in your care

• you were raised in a single-parent home

• you are presently a single parent

• you were raised in a family with a physically or mentally handicapped sibling or parent

• you now have a physically or mentally handicapped child in your home.

2. What percentage of your class raised a hand for at least one of the categories above?

What does this tell you about the importance of understanding principles for disciplining special children (adopted, foster, step, handicapped)?

Probing the Text (35–40 min.)

3. In Chapters 22 and 23 the Moores focus on the special discipline needs of adopted, foster, step, and handicapped children. Read aloud the paragraph in the middle of page 180 which begins: "All children deserve love."

What are some of the "circumstances" which have "betrayed" these special children?

In what ways do parents of special children, and the families and friends of these parents, add their betrayal to the circumstances?

4. Read Deuteronomy 10:17–19 and James 1:27 aloud.

What do these verses tell you about God's attitude toward special children and fractured families?

What is our scriptural responsibility to these people?

The Moores write, "Whether or not we are a part of these happenings, almost all of us have nearby friends who are, and it becomes us to be compassionate, appreciative, encouraging neighbors both to parents and children" (p. 183).

In what ways can we express compassion, appreciation, and encouragement toward special children who are not in our immediate families?

5. Review the eight lessons for stepparents on pages 186 and 187. Have stepparents in your class respond to each lesson by completing one of the following statements: "I have already practiced this lesson with my special children by . . ."; "I need to practice this lesson with my special children by . . ." Brainstorm specific activities stepparents can employ in applying these lessons.

6. The Moores say, "Most handicapped children—including the blind, deaf, and spastic—are generally underchallenged. They, like normal people, like to feel as normal as possible, and this feeling is best cultivated by helping them to be useful" (p. 192).

Why do most parents and friends of handicapped children fail to challenge them adequately?

Do you find yourself withholding patience, understanding, and love instead of generously sharing these qualities with the handicapped children you know?

What needs to happen before you are free to help the special children in your life feel as normal as possible?

7. In Chapter 24 the authors examine the contribution that fuzzy sex roles have made to family discipline problems. They write, "One of the most serious obstacles to family harmony and sensible child behavior and control, especially *self-control,* is the difference in relative maturity between boys and girls. Yet the basic reason for serious problems in most cases is simply that parents give little or no attention to these differences because they either do not know or don't care" (p. 193).

What are the differences the Moores were referring to (see pp. 194–198)?

What effect does a parent's irresponsibility in occupying properly his or her sex role have on these differences?

8. The Moores believe that "a powerful home-school renaissance" (p. 200) bodes well for a society which has pushed boys and girls into institutional education before they were mature enough to handle it. "But," they continue, "whether or not you educate your children formally at home, make sure that by precept and example you give them the most important education of all: creative minds, noble spirits, and honest souls" (p. 202).

What are some practical ways parents can help provide the three-fold education the Moores talk about if they home-school their children? if they institutionalize their children?

What advantages do you feel you bring to the method of education you have chosen for your children? what disadvantages?

Applying the Truth (10 min.)

9. Write a brief prayer in your notebook expressing to God the needs you feel as a result of today's discussion.

What is your growing edge regarding the special children in your family or in other families you know?

What are your concerns about the differences between your son(s) and daughter(s) and the pressures society places on them to conform or rebel? Express them to God in a few brief lines.

Gather with a few other class members and read your prayers to God in one another's hearing.

Assignment

Read Chapter 25 and the Afterword in *Home Built Discipline*.

Session 13

"Creative Punishment"
Chapter 25 and the Afterword

Getting Started (10 min.)

1. Share some experiences of punishment from your childhood by commenting on at least one of the following topics:

- a time you were punished for something you didn't do
- a time you escaped punishment for something you did do
- the form of punishment you dreaded most
- the form of punishment you dreaded least
- the "rod" used in your home for corporal punishment.

Probing the Text (40 min.)

2. The Moores state that discipline is primarily the fine art of discipleship, and should not be equated with punishment. "Yet there comes a time in nearly all children's lives," the authors continue, "when you have to 'take them in hand'" through creative punishment (p. 204). After reading Chapter 25, how would you define the term "creative punishment"? At what levels can creativity be exercised effectively in punishment? (See the examples on page 203 for ideas.)

3. Setting boundaries for a child's behavior is critical to fair punishment. Read aloud the paragraph at the bottom of page 204 which begins, "Have you consistently and reasonably set their boundaries?" Brainstorm specific areas in which boundaries need to be established (e.g., schedule, eating habits, playmates, television viewing, etc.).

What criteria for boundaries do you think should be generally observed in all Christian families?

What criteria for boundaries are unique to individual families?

4. Review the paragraphs on pages 205 and 206 under the heading "Corporal Punishment." As you talk through these paragraphs, compose a list of guidelines—specific do's and don'ts—for parents who administer corporal punishment. For example, you may determine from the first paragraph: always punish in love; always question your motives before acting. Write the guidelines for all to see.

5. Read aloud several verses from Proverbs which comment on the use of the rod (punishment through physical pain): 13:24; 22:15; 23:13; 29:15.

Which guidelines from the list in step 4 do these verses corroborate and amplify?

Which guidelines, if any, do these verses alter or negate?

What additional guidelines can you add to your list after reading these verses?

6. The Moores warn, *"The worst form of parenting . . . is to know what is right and not do it regardless of price"* (p. 206).

How difficult is it for you to consistently do the right thing in administering punishment?

What does it "cost" you to do the right thing; what personal effort, pain or planning accompanies those times when you must follow through with proper punishment?

7. The Moores stress the importance of a solid value system behind a parent's plan for punishment: "If you try to make decisions with young lives without reference to a consistent system of values, you will have little or no constructive discipline at all" (p. 207).

What specific resources have contributed to the forming of your parenting values (the Bible, denominational teaching, contemporary Christian books and tapes on parenting)?

What percentage of your value system have you accepted from others with little or no question?

What percentage have you hammered out through your own thought and study? (For example, are your children being educated institutionally because you have weighed the choices or because most every other family you know sends their young children to school?)

To what extent do you need to rethink your values on parenting?

8. The authors repeatedly return to the Golden Rule (Matt. 7:12) as a guideline for parenting, discipline, and punishment.

Do you punish your children similarly to the way you were punished as a child? If not, how are the two styles different?

Is your style of punishment commensurate with a style you would agree with if you were the child? If not, how could you alter your style to fit how you would like punishment administered to you?

9. There will be some times you administer needed punishment "with the certain risk that you will be seen as brutal, unmerciful, cruel, even evil" (p. 211).

How do you feel when you receive (or perceive) accusations like these from your child, your spouse, other adults, or your conscience?

To what extent are you tempted to compromise your punishment plan when these accusations arise?

To whom can you turn for encouragement, counsel, and support in these situations?

Applying the Truth (10 min.)

10. Review the guidelines for administering punishment which you listed during steps 4 and 5 above. Select two or three which you especially need to focus on prayerfully and apply to your program of discipline in the coming weeks. Write these guidelines in your notebook as goals, beginning with the words, "As God gives me wisdom and strength, I will . . . ."

11. Pray with at least one other person about the goals you have written. If appropriate, make a covenant with another class member or couple to support each other in prayer for the coming month as you seek to apply your insights from this thirteen-session class.

Retreat Ideas

The following pages contain a general outline for a parents' retreat based on portions of *Home Built Discipline*. The retreat is designed to begin with a Friday evening session and conclude with a Sunday morning worship service. You will notice that some time limits are given, but these may be adjusted to suit the needs of your particular group.

It is difficult to thoroughly cover an entire book in one weekend, because the study sessions must be combined into shorter time periods. This retreat assumes that the participants have read the book at least once prior to the weekend. Your group may consider using this retreat as a six- or twelve-month "check-up" to the thirteen-week study. This can be a time to refresh your collective memory about the ideas and resolutions that the group made earlier.

Although the group attending your retreat may be any size, large or small, much of the learning will take place in smaller groups. If you find that a large number of people will be attending the retreat, recruit a few people ahead of time to study the session plans prior to the weekend and act as discussion leaders. During the retreat, you may want to divide the group in different ways for each of the discussions in order to allow all the retreat participants to intermingle.

The retreat plans will work best if each person has his or her own copy of *Home Built Discipline* to use during the retreat. In addition, each person should bring his or her current spiritual journal or a small notebook to use as a retreat journal.

Again, this plan is a suggestion and should be adapted to your group's needs. Be sensitive to the issues being discussed and allow some flexibility in your schedule.

Friday Evening

(You should plan on meeting at approximately 7:00 or 7:30 P.M.)

Opening prayer

Speaker (30 min.): An encouraging testimony of God's help in parenting and discipline, preferably from an individual or couple in your church with a "track record" of successful parenting

Refreshments (20 min.)

Small group discussion (60–70 min.): Sessions 1 and 2 from *Home Built Discipline* study guide, "More than Punishment" and "A Pattern to Follow"

Saturday Morning

Breakfast (45 min.) at approximately 8:30 A.M.

Group singing and opening prayer (20 min.)

Small group discussion (60–70 min.): Sessions 3 and 5, "A Creative Approach" and "What Makes Your Child Tick?"

Break (20 min.)

Small group discussion (60–70 min.): Sessions 4 and 6, "Parental Control Develops Self-Control" and "Example and Order"

Lunch (45 min.)

Saturday Afternoon

Games and recreation (1¹/₂ hrs.)

Group singing and testimonies (20 min.)

Small group discussion (60–70 min.): Sessions 7, 8, and 9, "Working, Playing, and Serving Together," "Involvement and Consistency," and "Prompting Thought and Giving Encouragement"

Break (20 min.)

Small group discussion (60–70 min.): Sessions 10 and 11, "Health and Money" and "Dealing with Putdowns and Down Times"

Break to relax and have dinner (1¹/₂ hrs.)

Saturday Evening

Group singing and prayer (20 min.)

Small group discussion (60–70 min.): Session 12, "Special Children and Boy/Girl Roles"

Refreshments (20 min.)

Small group discussion (60–70 min.): Session 13, "Creative Punishment"

You will finish this final session between 9:00 and 9:30 P.M. You want to plan a time of humorous skits or a talent show for the late evening.

Sunday Morning

Breakfast (45 min.) at approximately 8:30 A.M.

Worship, hymn-singing, group prayer, sharing (45 min.)

Speaker (30 min.): Leader or Friday-night speaker may talk with the large group and tie together the themes that have been discussed, important applications the group has discovered, etc.

Closing prayer

Break to pack and leave retreat area by approximately 11:30 A.M.

Notes

Chapter 3

1. Lee Canter and Marlene Canter, *Assertive Discipline* (Canter & Associates, 1976).
2. Rudolf Dreikurs, *Encouraging Children to Learn* (1963).
3. Thomas Gordon, *T.E.T. Teacher Effectiveness Training* (P. H. Wyden, 1974).
4. See Stanley Milgram, "Behavioral Study of Obedience," *Journal of Abnormal and Social Psychology* (1953): 371-8. Also see Don Hammachek, "Removing the Stigma from Obedience Behavior," *Phi Delta Kappan* (March 1976); Jack Canfield and Harold Wells, *100 Ways to Enhance Self-Concept in the Classroom* (Englewood Cliffs, N.J.: Prentice-Hall, 1967). Canfield and Wells offer a large assortment of activities to promote self-esteem.
5. See Marilyn Kash and Gary Borick, *Teacher Behavior and Pupil Self-Concept* (Addison Wesley, 1978).
6. See Arthur Jersild, *When Teachers Face Themselves* (Teacher's College Press, 1955).

Chapter 4

1. R. S. Moore and Dorothy Moore, *Home Made Health* (Waco, Tex.: Word, 1980).
2. Moore and Moore, *Home Grown Kids* (Waco, Tex.: Word, 1981).
3. Ibid. Also see the Afterword.

Chapter 7

1. James L. Hymes, *Teaching the Child Under Six* (Columbus, Ohio: Merrill, 1968).
2. The best we have found is The Winston Grammar Game. For information, send a self-addressed, stamped envelope to The Moore Foundation, Box 1, Camas, Wash. 98607.
3. For documentation, see Moore and Moore, *Better Late Than Early* (Hewitt Research, 1975) and *School Can Wait* (Hewitt Research, 1979). For information, send a self-addressed, stamped envelope to Box 1, Camas, Wash. 98607.
4. Moore and Moore, *Better Late Than Early* and *School Can Wait;* "Research and Common Sense," *Teacher's College Record* (Winter 1982-3). For information on these and other documents, send a self-addressed, stamped envelope to Box 1, Camas, Wash. 98607.

Chapter 8

1. Anne K. Soderman, "Schooling All 4-Year-Olds: An Idea Full of Promise, Fraught with Pitfalls," *Education Week* (March 14, 1984), p. 19.
2. For full information on Christian education materials on sex, send a self-addressed, stamped envelope to Box 1, Camas, Wash. 98607.

Chapter 9
1. Harold G. McCurdy, "The Childhood Pattern of Genius," *Horizon* 3 (May 1960): 33-8.
2. John I. Goodlad, "A Study of Schooling: Some Findings and Hypotheses," *Phi Delta Kappan* 64 (March 1983), p. 7.
3. McCurdy, op. cit.

Chapter 11
1. M. E. Sadler, ed., *Moral Instruction and Training in the Schools* (New York: Longmans, Green and Co., 1908), p. 94.
2. William D. Rohwer, Jr., "Prime Time for Education: Early Childhood or Adolescence?" *Harvard Educational Review,* 41 (1971), p. 336. See also the address presented at the annual meeting of the American Educational Research Association, New Orleans, 1973: "Improving Instruction in the 1970s—What Could Make a Significant Difference?" and "Inequality in School Success: The Neglect of Individuals" at the Thirteenth Annual NEA Conference on Civil and Human Rights Project 1975: Educational Neglect. Washington Hilton Hotel, February 15-18, 1975.
3. For more information, including lists of common family industries, read the authors' book, *Home Style Teaching.* Also see your librarian for books on cottage industries.

Chapter 13
1. Peter Uhlenberg and David Eggebeen, paper presented at meeting of the Family Research Council, George Washington University, Wash., D.C., June 12-14, 1986.

Chapter 15
1. McCurdy, op. cit.

Chapter 17
1. For fully documented treatment of family health, including this chapter and other chapters on health, and for more background on statements in this chapter, see Moore and Moore, *Home Made Health.*
2. Tufts University, *Diet and Nutrition News Letter* 3 (November 1985).

Chapter 19
1. Raymond S. Moore, et al., *Influences on Learning in Early Childhood,* prepared for the U.S. Office of Economic Opportunity under Research Grant No. 50079-G-73/1 (Berrien Springs, Mich., 1975, mimeograph).
2. McCurdy, op. cit.
3. In a speech to Spokane College Women's Club, 1979.
4. Martin Engel, "Rapunzel, Rapunzel, Let Down Your Golden Hair: Some Thoughts on Early Childhood Education," unpublished manuscript, National Demonstration Center in Early Childhood Education, U.S. Office of Education, Wash., D.C.
5. Urie Bronfenbrenner, *Two Worlds of Childhood: U.S. and U.S.S.R.* (New York: Simon & Schuster, 1970), p. 97.

6. In *All Our Children Learning* (McGraw-Hill, 1980).

7. Glen P. Nimnicht, as quoted by Betty Hannah Hoffman, "Do You Know How to Play with Your Child?" *Woman's Day,* August 1972, pp. 46, 118. Confirmed by personal letter from Dr. Nimnicht, September 29, 1972.

Chapter 21

1. J. T. Fisher, *A Few Buttons Missing* (Philadelphia: Lippincott, 1951), p. 273.

Chapter 24

1. Carle Zimmerman, *Family and Civilization* (New York: Harper, 1947).

2. In "The Primary Education Fetish" Forum (1898), vol. 25, pp. 314–328.

3. Dept. of Health, Education, and Welfare, Behavior Patterns of Children in School, publication no. (HRA)76–1042 (February 1972), p. 12.

4. Soderman, op. cit.

Afterword

1. For more complete treatment, see Moore and Moore, *Home Made Health*.

Index

252

254

255

For Further Information

For further information on The Moore Foundation on home-based education or on others of the authors' books, send a self-addressed, stamped envelope to PO Box 1, Camas, Wash. 98706.